POLISH PROFILES

*The Land, the People
and
Their History*

All poetry in this volume was written by the author
or translated into English by him.

Other Books by Antoni Gronowicz

Other Books by Antoni Gronowicz

BIOGRAPHIES

Béla Schick and the World of Children
Chopin
Gallant General
Modjeska: Her Life and Loves
Paderewski
Rachmaninoff
Tchaikovsky

NOVELS

Bolek
Four from the Old Town
Hitler's Woman
The Hookmen
An Orange Full of Dreams

PLAYS

Chiseler's Paradise
Forward Together
Greta
The United Animals

POETRY

Polish Poems
The Quiet Vengeance of Words

ESSAYS

Pattern for Peace
The Piasts

W. Wilanowski (left), president of the Polish airline LOT, celebrates the inauguration of service between New York and Warsaw, April 16, 1973. With him are (l. to r.) Dr. E. Kusielewicz, president of the Kosciuszko Foundation in New York, a stewardess, and Z. Stabeusz, director of LOT's New York offices.

POLISH PROFILES

The Land, the People

and

their History

ANTONI GRONOWICZ

LAWRENCE HILL & COMPANY
Westport, Connecticut

Library of Congress Cataloging in Publication Data

Gronowicz, Antoni, 1913–

Polish Profiles.

1. Poland.

I. Title.

DK4040.G76   943.8   75–23929

ISBN 0–88208–060–1

Library of Congress Catalog Card Number: 75-23929

ISBN: 0-88208-060-1

First edition, May, 1976

Lawrence Hill & Co., Publishers, Inc.
Manufactured in the United States of America by
RAY FREIMAN & COMPANY

to the memory of my
Christian and Jewish friends
who died during the Second World War

Table of Contents

Prologue

Prologue

There is no land from which I will not yearn
For the former, dusky streets.
Every victorious cry will break in sorrow and turn
To where ancientness meets.

There is no land which I could prize
Without that greyed antiquated reminiscence,
Everywhere, everywhere my eyes
Are only for gazing, not for the senses.

Nothing, nothing can calm me in lands,
Nothing on an impulse will any longer hold me.
Always with an aperture over me stands
Heaven—the earth, my family.
No journeys can help the heart's hunger
Nor multitudes, nor oceans.
I meditate on the streets each time a little longer,
Contemplating, listening, listening to these potions.

The most exquisite words cannot rain
Nor savage hymns, nor crazed races.
Whatsoever will be—they will return again
The immemorial, daily prayers, like stars to their places.
I call, I call, I wring my hands despairingly,
Lord, hear me out; light up the heavens with a sword!
And he—there, on the street, he waits for me:
My acquaintance, a good simple man of his word.

    My friend Julian Tuwim has expressed with this poem my
precise sentiments.

I write as I see. If I cannot write the truth, I prefer to be silent. I believe that such a viewpoint serves the idea of justice and the betterment of society, even though historical and social truths may be seen subjectively.

I was born on Polish soil into a backward peasant society steeped in rigid Roman Catholicism. I did not acquire my first pair of shoes until I was eleven years old, and these were secondhand. There were class obstacles to self-advancement, but I was strong and I took all that I could, even a university education. The Polish soil was good to me, but some people, especially government officials, were not. My real struggle began when I decided to become a writer, for my consciousness had been formed from work with the soil and from knowledge and love of my country's long, rich tradition, and not from exploitation of another's labor. The struggle was sometimes rewarding, sometimes bitter, often disappointing, and ultimately sorrowful. Feeling trapped, and overcome by frustration mingled with premonition of my own imminent destruction, I left my native land in 1938. I don't know what would have happened to me if I had remained. A year later, Nazi hordes began their slaughter of my people and the devastation of my country.

I arrived in New York City. Despite many difficulties, I became an American writer.

The country I had left became the inspiration for much of my writing. Its people had waged a long, hard battle for a better material and social existence, but it was only after the Second World War, when Poland became the Polish People's Republic, that the goal became a reality. I visited my reborn country for the first time in 1963 and by 1975 had returned six times. So the pages of this book are based on my own observations of Poland over the last twelve years and an intimate knowledge of her earlier history.

Today, Poland has about thirty-four million people living on 120,725 square miles. Globally, she ranks sixty-first in territory and twenty-first in population. On the north lies the Baltic Sea and on the south the picturesque Carpathian Mountains that rise up to become the border between Poland and Czechoslovakia. On the east is the Soviet Union while on the west is the German Democratic Republic. The Polish population is 98 percent Roman Catholic. The remaining 2 percent is comprised of Greek Orthodox, Jewish, Protestant, and smaller religious groupings. Before the war Poland was home for as many Jews proportionately to the population as there are blacks or Italians in the United States today. The Nazis exterminated two million of them along with four million Christians, for a total of six million Poles. Twenty million Soviet citizens also perished.

Poland relies on the East, rather than the West, for protection, guidance, and development. This will be the case so long as there is a Germany that refuses to commemorate the thirtieth anniversary of the overthrow of Hitler (as the West German government refused to do this past year), and so long as the West German government persists in rearming at her present frightening pace and in allowing former Nazis and their sympathizers to occupy high positions in her society.

Since the war, Poland has almost tripled her gross national income. Fifty-five percent of this income is derived from mining, chemicals, machine manufacturing, and power production; 20 percent from agriculture; 15 percent from finance and services; and 10 percent from commerce.

The legislative body is unicameral and consists of 460 members who are elected every four years. There are three major political parties: the Democratic Party, the United Peasants' Party, and the Polish United Workers' Party. The last-named is the dominant political organization, both in numbers and in influence. Its First Secretary ranks higher than the president, whose official title is Chairman of the Council of the State. Third in power is the Chairman of the Council of Ministers.

When I returned to Poland for the first time in 1963, the First Secretary was Wladyslaw Gomulka. He had reached this office seven years earlier as a result of the de-Stalinization of Eastern Europe which commenced with Khrushchev's 1956 speech denouncing the deceased Soviet leader. Gomulka had been prosecuted before the Second World War by the then Polish governments, hunted by the Gestapo during the Nazi occupation, and was under house arrest for a short time under the Stalinist regime of Boleslaw Bierut.

In the middle 1950s after Stalin's death, strikes and demonstrations occurred in many Polish cities. June 1956 brought riots to the city of Poznan, which eventually led to the October "bloodless revolution" and to Gomulka's assumption of power.

The new party leader was born on February 6, 1905, in Krosno, a city located in Poland's southern oil-field region between Cracow and Lwow. Earlier, his parents, Jan and Kunegunda, had tried their luck in the United States. Jan worked as a coal miner and their two daughters were born there. But they could not accustom themselves to the American way of life and so, a year before Wladyslaw was born, they returned to Krosno where Jan became an oil worker.

Their son Wladyslaw attended the local public school where he was an average student. He received most of his education, however, from his voracious reading of books. From early youth he was radical and participated in various social and political causes. By his early twenties he had become a revolutionary. From my own observation, as well as that of colleagues who worked closely with him along various stages of his career, Gomulka can be labeled a typical Polish peasant, honest and hardworking, stubborn—perhaps too much so—and suspicious, especially of intellectuals. While in office his capacity for work was surpassed only by his love for Poland. Once he told me, "I want to make Poland a just, socialist country in my lifetime."

Gomulka's attempts to reshape Poland met with many difficulties, as the following anecdote, which he was fond of telling, indicates:

> Once I made a speech to a group of peasants in which I tried to tell them something about the continuity of socialist thought. I said that Marx took the grain from Hegel and left the chaff. After the meeting was over one of the peasants approached me to ask, "Comrade Gomulka, please tell me, in secret of course, how many years did this Marx get for stealing the grain?"

Upon his election as First Secretary, Gomulka adopted as his slogan, "Every nation builds her own socialism." In the place of forced collectivization of farms he instituted a program of intensive political education which was designed to persuade the peasants to join the collectives voluntarily. In the factories, workers were given more freedom in planning production and work schedules. Such decentralizing tactics helped to give the producers a sense of ownership and direct participation in raising production. Even the intellectuals, whom he never trusted, were given a share in building socialism.

In religious matters, Gomulka was as tolerant and pragmatic as the fifteenth-century bishop of Cracow who said, "My dear parishoners, you may believe in a goat if you want to, but you must pay taxes to the Church." Gomulka considered religion a private matter that had no place in state affairs. At the same time, he advocated that the state should not take too severe a stance against organized religion. Toward this end, he reopened communications with the Roman Catholic Church in an attempt to improve relations.

His lifelong fight against anti-Semitism, perhaps given more impetus by the fact that his wife Sophie was Jewish, showed positive results during his term of office. While he was party leader, Jews occupied proportionally more positions than Roman Catholics in all economic, political, and cultural activities. Dr. Eugeniusz Szyr, the Deputy Prime Minister, was Jewish, as was the then, and now, Minister of Railroads. The foreign affairs, domestic and foreign trade, education, and interior ministries were staffed, and continue to be staffed, by Jews. The only government-supported Jewish theater in the world outside of Israel is in Warsaw, and it was built under Gomulka; it performs Yiddish classics the year round. The theater itself costs the government four million *zlotys* a year to run, an amount that the American government would spend if it assumed the yearly running costs of a large Broadway theater. A weekly newspaper in Yiddish was subsidized with three million *zlotys* annually until the Six Day War between the Arabs and the Israelis in 1967. At that time, many Jews emigrated to Israel, and the readership so diminished that it was no longer practical to continue publication. However, a monthly is still being published and continues to be subsidized by the government.

Until the Six Day War, Poland had normal diplomatic, cultural, and economic relations with Israel. She then joined many other countries in Africa, Asia, and Eastern Europe in withdrawing formal diplomatic recognition. Jews in sensitive government positions who had expressed pro-Israeli feelings were demoted. Others decided to leave the country and to fight to preserve Israel's independence. They encountered no difficulty in obtaining passports or in exchanging *zlotys* into foreign currency for traveling. The exodus of 10,000 Jews bewildered many Poles who neither understood nor appreciated this sudden, active manifestation of support for another country.

In the meantime, opposition to Gomulka's leadership began to grow. At first, it was led either by those intellectuals who favored Stalinist methods and attacked his "socialist sovereignty" program as a form of Titoism, or by those who desired a return to Western-style democracy and worked underground against him. It proliferated, however, until it touched all segments of the population. Such opposition took place in the midst of a general rise in the standard of living, more freedom for the mass of the population, and increased industrial and agricultural production.

As the pressure from inside and outside his regime increased, Gomulka's *modus operandi* appeared to change. He began avoiding people. Then he ceased making speeches altogether and confined his contacts with workers and peasants to national holiday celebrations and party functions. He had lost touch with the needs and desires of the people. Surrounding Gomulka were yes-men who submitted overly optimistic reports, which he naively took at face value.

The gulf between the bureaucracy and the working classes was noticeable everywhere. During a visit in the summer of 1969, I took a trolley from the center of Warsaw to the Praga district. When I got on, the conductor was yelling at the passengers, "Gentlemen, don't block the exits."

"Mister Conductor," one of the riders yelled back, "don't call us gentlemen. We are all comrades."

A second rider corrected him, "I see no comrades here. They're all riding in chauffered limousines."

Gomulka's failure in part was caused by the mistaken notion that he could transform an agricultural Poland into a modern industrial socialist country in one generation. It was only in 1966 that the number of people living in urban areas surpassed those living in the countryside. An additional failing was his strong distrust of intellectuals on principle. Without a tremendous emphasis on education and support for the intellectuals who serve it, you cannot have socialism.

Gomulka's fall from power came on the heels of a critical situation which developed on December 14 and 15, 1970, when workers in Gdansk and Szczecin demonstrated against a sudden increase in the prices of food, clothing, and other commodities. As First Secretary, Gomulka was most responsible for this ill-timed government edict issued just before the Christmas holidays. "When the king makes a mistake, the nation has to pay," said the poet Horace. The revolt spread to other cities on the northern coast, and by its end over one hundred workers had died from the bullets of the Polish police.

Gomulka's only response to the crisis, as reported by the people closest to him, was to weep and to bewail, over and over, that the nation had betrayed him. On December 20, the Central Committee of the United Workers' Party accepted his resignation as First Secretary and as member of the Political Bureau and formally wished him a "speedy recovery." (The rumor had now spread that he had all along been suffering from arterial sclerosis.)

That same day, the party selected Edward Gierek as First Secretary, a man with a realistic planner's ability founded upon a solid technical education. He was born on January 6, 1913, into a miner's family in Porabka in Bedzin county. After his father died in a mine accident in 1922, Gierek emigrated to France with his mother. Unlike Gomulka, he spent many of his early years outside of Poland accustoming himself to the different economic and social circumstances he found abroad. When he was thirteen, he began working in the French coal mines and took part in the union movement. In 1931, he became a member of the French Communist Party and was active in strikes and worker education. Three years later, he was arrested by the French police and was deported to Poland. In 1937, he went to Belgium to work in the mines there. Before the Second World War, both France and Belgium traditionally provided employment for Poles. The mines at this time were seething with political discontent, and it was here that Gierek found his spiritual home.

During the war he fought the Nazis as a member of the Belgian Communist Party. After the war he became chief organizer in Belgium for the Polish Workers' Party. In 1948, after seventeen years in the mines, he returned to Poland to become an official of the Central Committee of the Polish Workers' Party. A year later, he became Secretary of the Executive Committee in Katowice, where he also received an engineer's degree in coal mining. In 1954, he was transferred to the Central Committee in charge of heavy industry. He became a member of the Political Bureau of the Central Committee in 1956, and finally, on December 20,1970, he was appointed to Poland's highest political office, First Secretary.

In accepting this highest position on a very sad day for Poland, Gierek said, "The recent tragic happenings in our country very painfully remind us that the party ought to maintain the closest relationship to the working class and the entire nation. We must analyze the roots of the national economic situation. We have to make only those reforms that yield dynamic and harmonious development. We trust our decisions will reflect the cooperation of the Peasants Party, the Democratic Party and all other groups within the United National Front to secure a just resolution to our problems."

He concluded, "A quarter of a century ago, our nation set out to build socialism. Although we went on this road after the most tragic events in our history, we have achieved a great deal by working together. We can do more, and we shall do more to open for the young generation new horizons on this road to socialism and prosperity.''

Action followed speeches and slogans. The price of food and other necessities was cut 10 percent. The social atmosphere became more relaxed. On radio and television, people openly discussed the reasons for the tragic occurrences of the previous December. Gierek went on a tour of Poland to explain the country's economic situation. He appealed for greater effort on farms and in factories to produce more goods for domestic consumption and for export. Once again the atmosphere was one of optimism— especially when stocks of foreign as well as domestic goods increased. An indication of the nation's newly found confidence was that jokes and sayings about Gierek mushroomed. One of the jokes was that in a few years every Polish family would have not a Volkswagen, but at least a *volkswagierek*. In my conversations with him in 1972, Gierek suggested that his economic plans are based on the necessity for capital goods production and the expansion of world market possibilities.

Gierek's managerial skills were apparent years ago, when during his tenure in Silesia, the chief coal mining province in Poland, he promoted increased coal production and closer relations between workers and government officials. As First Secretary, these skills have been put to good use. In addition, his constant traveling about the country has helped create an air of confidence and unity among the people.

At the invitation of President Gerald Ford, Gierek visited the United States for six days beginning October 8, 1974. According to the American press, he conveyed both sincerity and statesmanship, and his visit was judged successful in fostering better relations with this country. In July, 1975, Ford came to Poland, and in September of that year it was announced that the General Motors Corporation planned to manufacture trucks in Poland for sale throughout the world.

During the past thirty years, Polish industry has finally realized its potential. Her industry had never developed earlier because of foreign capitalist control of investment and the anti-

First Secretary Edward Gierek initiates a construction project on National Labor Day.

Gierek visited the United States at the invitation of President Ford, arriving on October 8, 1974.

1608 1958
FIRST POLES
LANDED IN JAMESTOWN, VIRGINIA
OCTOBER 1, 1608
ARRIVED ABOARD BRITISH SAILER
"MARY AND MARGARET"
MICHAL LOWICKI   ZBIGNIEW STEFANSKI
JAN BOGDAN   JAN MATA
STANISLAW SADOWSKI
DONATED BY
THE POLISH FALCONS OF AMERICA

The First Secretary and his wife admire a plaque commemorating the landing of the first Polish settlers in Jamestown, Virginia.

industrial bias of the *szlachta* (the landed gentry). Before the war, Poland's per capita industrial activity was four-fifths the world average and many times below the average of France, England, and Germany; now her output is well over twice the world average and 90 percent of these Western nations'. Starting in 1946, Poland's rate of industrial growth was one of the three highest in the world. This process has not abated during the 1970s. Actual industrial production in 1975 was nine times higher than it was in 1950, while world production rose only 3.5 times within the same period. In output Poland now ranks tenth among the world's nations.

In world production of coal Poland is fourth, in sulphur, fishing vessels, and freight cars third, and in machinery for road building and houses eighth. She also ranks higher than most of the industrial countries in rate of modernization. Poland has devoted much productive energy to rebuilding her mining industry, so that in 1975 anthracite production surpassed 162 million tons. Shipbuilding also expanded, with the result that, in 1975, 101 ocean-going vessels totaling 670,000 tons were overhauled. The Polish auto industry, nonexistent in 1946, was, by 1975, producing 165,000 passenger cars and tens of thousands of buses and other special vehicles. The modernized petrochemical and electronic industries do not merely fulfill the nation's needs; they are making products for export as well.

The best evidence of Poland's rising standard of living is that real income has increased 40 percent since 1970. Between 1951 and 1972, only Rumania, Bulgaria, the U.S.S.R., and Japan experienced a higher rate of growth in national income. This higher standard of living was possible only through the great sacrifices of her people and in spite of the fact that the first years of socialism took place under the most difficult of conditions—the legacy of a horrible war, together with some resistance to the new ideas of political and social organization that were being introduced.

During my last visit in 1975, the differences in housing between Poland and middle-class districts in Western Europe were no longer noticeable. However, I still found weaknesses in ser-

vices. When I asked one high official why the service industry had
not improved, he responded, "In our country, whether you work
or not, you still get a guaranteed income. Only improved education
and greater self-discipline will develop a higher sense of responsibility in each citizen."

Many, especially in the West, have questioned the desirabil-
ity of the state providing its citizens with all that is necessary for
basic existence. Indeed, some irresponsible individuals do take
advantage of the situation and do not contribute their share to the
general welfare. But those who question must ponder the far
greater evil of beggars, prostitutes, and the deprived aged living in
the streets of Western countries.

Traveling has taught me much. It has certainly enriched my
imagination. Traveling in Poland has done much more: it has
enriched my soul.

PART I

Chapter 1

o
dawn in multiple
scent
and
color
coring day
why are we thus induced
to hope again
only
to
see
our hopes traduced
our dreams
in scarlet mist burning away
watch out
i
will
bring
suit
against this treachery
and
you will lose
and
god will have to pay

At exactly 3:47 on the morning of October 13, 1946, an enormously long freight train started pulling slowly out of the station in Lublin. It was headed west, bound for the city of Jelenia Gora in Lower Silesia. This train was laden with human beings, baggage, agricultural implements, factory machinery, and farm animals. The grinding of wheels, the noise made by the people and the animals, the tooting of the whistle, and the puffing of the engine all created a cacophony that rolled in echoes over the flat fields on either side of the tracks. It was the farewell song for those who were leaving central and eastern Poland to return to their former homes in the west. They were going back to the Nisa and Oder to begin a new, more tranquil life.

Since the second half of 1945, many such trains had been making their way across Poland to Pomerania, Lubusz, and Silesia. Some of the passengers were returning to the homes from which they had been ousted by the Nazis after September, 1939. Others were from overcrowded sectors of central Poland, France, and Belgium.

The victorious Allies had shifted the eastern boundary of Poland to the Curzon Line. They had also determined that the western borders of the country would be restored to the line formed by the Nisa and Oder rivers and the Baltic Sea. In this way, Poland became united geographically and ethnologically and was in a measure compensated for the losses she had suffered in the Second World War.

The resources of these western territories would become the prerequisites for the continued existence and sound development of the nation in the second half of the twentieth century. In defense of this region, thousands of Polish soldiers had died on the Nisa and the Oder and on the Pomeranian fronts in the war, just as their ancestors before them in numerous wars dating back to the Middle Ages. For Slavs, the progenitors of the present-day Poles, have inhabited this territory since before recorded history. These regions belonged to Poland and had been successfully defended against the German push to the east—the *Drang nach Osten*. It was Poles, not Germans, who long ago converted the pagans to Christianity in the territory east of the Oder, on the Baltic, and in the Pomeranian provinces. It was Poles, not Germans, who founded the first bishoprics in cities like Kolobrzeg, Lubusz, and Wroclaw.

It was only in comparatively modern times, a short time before the first partition of Poland, in 1772, that Poland lost these western lands. Even when the Poles lost their independence, they never gave up the idea of recovering this land and regaining freedom. Some of the most famous Polish writers kept this indomitable spirit alive in Polish literature, with the result that during the almost 150-year occupation there were numerous insurrections against the Germans in this territory. In the past, Poland's development was seriously hampered by the loss of her western territories. From a geographical and strategical viewpoint, they are as vital to Poland as the English Channel is to Great Britain or the Rhine to France.

In returning territory that included the banks of the Oder, the German capitalists and militarists lost not only land and industrial potential, but also a convenient springboard for a possible future attack on the whole of southeastern and eastern Europe. The border lands running from the bend of the Sudeten slightly to the west from the course of the Lusatian Nisa River up to the Gulf of Szczecin constitute the shortest possible line separating Germany from the spacious plains inhabited by the Slavs. This line is defended on the south by the mighty range of mountains that begins at the Sudety and ends in the Swiss Alps. In the north, this vital line is defended by the Gulf of Szczecin. If there was any place where Germany's drive to the east could have been stopped, it was there; it was on this strategic frontier that Poland's territories were resecured.

Quite naturally, then, plans to rebuild the country after the Second World War centered on these regained western territories with their fertile farm lands and rich deposits of coal, iron, zinc, potassium, and oil, all of which were necessary for national self-sufficiency. On the basis of the richness of these territories, the so-called Three-Year Plan for Polish Reconstruction came into being in 1945. The primary goal of this plan was to raise the standard of living of the exhausted population, which could no longer exist under scarcity conditions. A nation on the brink of limitless despair had to have hope restored and be nursed daily with larger rations of food and clothing. Most importantly, it was necessary to mobilize the widest strata of the population to mine the iron, zinc, and coal and exchange these resources abroad for factory equipment, farm implements, and other necessities. Public and technical schools were built to educate specialists as quickly as possible, for, among the first, the Nazis had murdered the scientists, professionals, and skilled technicians.

(German statistics of May 17, 1939, revealed that the western territories were inhabited by 8.2 million Germans, of whom over a million were of Polish origin.) In 1945, after the cessation of hostilities, a spontaneous influx of Poles began into these regions. On February 14, 1946, 2.9 million Poles were already there; in 1947, 5 million; and, in 1970, 9 million. The number of Germans, on the other hand, shrank to 120,000. Today 88 percent of the population of the western territories is younger than 30. This generation was born there.

(According to the Potsdam Agreement in 1945, the Allies were to expatriate from the Polish western territories 2 million Germans to the Soviet sector and 1.5 million to the English part of Germany. The others had been evacuated with the retreating Nazi armies or were to leave Silesia, the region of Lubusz, Pomerania, and Eastern Prussia a few months later.) While this migration was taking place, Poles from the overpopulated central part and from Western Europe were converging daily by the thousands upon the Nisa, the Oder, and the Baltic. There were Polish soldiers from England and Italy, as well as Polish civilians from all over the world—among them peasants, tradesmen, artisans, officials, and professional people, all with their belongings and their dreams for the future. They immediately undertook the restoration of the cities, factories, and farms. In 1947, of the 4.5 million hectares of arable land in this region, 3.8 million were seeded.

The exiles who were now returning to their homes in the western territories and the newcomers to these lands experienced many problems of adjustment. My childhood friend Bronislaw Wiernik, who is an elementary school teacher, recounted many incidents of cultural difficulties. He told me of one man who came west from behind the Curzon Line, where he had lived in a mud hut, and of how he could not get used to the electric lights he found on the Oder. There was also the story of the public school class in Lower Silesia where a fourteen-year-old boy from central Poland told a man from northern France: "You are a Frenchie, and not a Pole!"

Indeed, not unexpectedly, the newcomers felt strange and lonely, and as a result many misunderstandings arose. Poles from east of the Curzon Line, central Poland, the French provinces, and the mines of Belgium, who had spent many years abroad or who had been living for some time in other parts of Poland, all had to become accustomed to their present environment and to one another. They had to have time to grow out of their old habits. They had to learn to stop making comparisons with their pasts.

They ridiculed one another, bragged about their own superiority, and incessantly debated the question as to which group had the greatest rights in Poland. Slight misunderstandings frequently exploded into serious arguments and open quarrels. So, in the beginning, they usually emerged from their parties and other gatherings in somber moods. Those from Silesia could not live in peace with those from France. People from central Poland could not get along with people from the "North."

While some were satisfied with their new lives, others, even some of the more patient members of the communities, became malcontents. Many complained bitterly that wages were too low and others that the living quarters allocated to their families were inadequate. This one did not get enough furniture; that one had not received her full quota of flour for the month. The Ksiaznice cooperative did not have enough rye. The cows were not in good condition and were plastered with dung. There were no movies, and the evenings were so long! And then there was that high-flown language: "I beg your pardon," and "Please excuse me," all day long, and the everlasting hand kissing. The worst offenders in this respect were the officers.

The greatest contention centered on the French migrants. The boys and girls who had been born in France and who spoke Polish with difficulty were ridiculed by the native Poles and were taunted with such epithets as "greenhorn." In turn, those who had lived in France frequently found their new way of life wanting. "In France, everything was taken care of at the one window in the *Grand Bureau*—so at the end of the day you were through. But here they say: 'Come back Monday.' Then on Monday they tell you to come Tuesday. And if a fellow so much as dares to open his mouth to complain about all this, he is told: 'Well, if you don't like it, why don't you go back to where you came from?' "

In such moments of anger, some of the Poles who had come from France forgot that they had come to work hard to help rebuild Poland and to raise her out of the ruins of war, not to live a life of ease and luxury. They had come of their own free will, and, in fact, efforts had even been made by anti-Socialists and church groups in France to keep them from going back at all. When the native-born Poles jeeringly asked them why they had migrated, some of the "foreigners" lost their tempers, and in their anger they themselves could not remember why they had returned.

In time, however, the problems of the newcomers began to disappear. Earlier, one woman had repeatedly avowed that she was going to return to France even if she had to walk back. Six months later, Bronislaw Wiernik said to her, "Well, madam, what do you say? Do you still want to hike back to France?" And she replied, "No, by Jesus and his Holy Mother, sticks and stones could not drive me out now."

Wiernik also spoke of the changes that had come over a group of "Frenchies" he had found digging potatoes on the road from Mietkow to Ksiaznice.

"How are you getting along?"

"Pretty well," they replied cheerfully, resting a minute on their shovels. "No more complaints!"

In the first cooperative of the French agrarian workers, the situation finally improved. After their first year, they told Bronislaw that after the harvest things would be much better than they were in France. In 1947, they harvested seven hactares of beets, which they exchanged in the sugar factory at Pustkow for 2,848 kilograms of sugar. That would last for two years and there would also be some left over to sell. They would exchange their oats for rye. Many had fattened pigs.

"The worst is over for me now," said one farmer. "I'll be on my feet by May. And the cows are not sickly any more, they are getting stronger all the time." Another man told Bronislaw that they were only workmen in France, but that here they were property owners.

In Walbrzych, Jedlina, Zdroj, Domowice, Pelcznica, Nowa Ruda, Kuznice Swiednickie, Sobiecin, Boguszow, Solice Dolne, Piastowo, Biskupice, Sosnica, Szombierki, Zabrze, Bytom, and Gliwice, Bronislaw went to his old friends the miners six months after they had arrived to ask them how they were getting along. He also questioned their wives and their children. "It was hard at first, but it has gotten a lot better," they answered. "We don't long for French wine any more. It was bitter, anyway." One woman responded that in France she had had to walk 15 kilometers for flour and had a difficult time trying to figure out every day what to cook for her 11 children. "I have so many sons," she said proudly, "to whom should I give them if not to Poland?"

"Our children," said the mothers, "were always so sickly in France, but here not one of them has had a cough all winter." They also spoke of the fun they had skiing in the mountains. The mountains did not appear strange to them anymore. Neither did the people.

In the town council of Ksiaznice, one of the counselors came from central Poland, one from France, and another from the east. The three worked hand-in-hand on all kind of committees and organizations and in their political parties. Schoolgirls from east of the Curzon Line and from France now sat together in class and became the best of friends. "Their differences have disappeared," said their teacher, a repatriate from Russia. And a fifteen-year-old who was born in France exclaimed, "At last, I feel like a Pole among Poles."

After two or three years, the "Belgian" and the "Frenchman" began to discover that they were compatriots, and the Silesians no longer complained.

"We made a grave mistake about those who came here from

abroad,'' apologized those from central Poland. ''Maybe it is true that they have not yet become a part of our difficult way of life here, but no wonder. They never had to live through what we did, so when they become impatient and demand what's coming to them, we do not blame them at all.''

Among those who came from Belgium and adapted to the new way of life was Wincenty Pstrowski. In Belgium he had lived in a five-room apartment; here he had only two small rooms for himself, his wife, and four children. All he said was: ''Whose fault is it? Can I blame poor, ruined Poland? Let's first build the country up again before we start complaining.'' Pstrowski has helped rebuild the country with his work in the Jadwiga mine. Almost from the very start in those early days he was able to produce 200 tons of coal and take 17,000 *zlotys* home to his two-room flat every month.

There were more such Pstrowskis. In the Krystyna mine, 345 meters underground, a group of miners from Belgium, France, Silesia, Boryslaw, and Poznan worked side by side at the same wall. It became like one big family reunion whose members, after having knocked about in every corner of the earth for many long years, finally came home for good.

It is clear that Poland's western border regions have greatly assisted her transformation from a totally agrarian economy to a well balanced agricultural, industrial, and commercial economy. Compared with prewar production, Poland now produces 240 percent more in the metallurgical field and 140 percent more in cement, coal, and electrical energy. In the production of zinc and textiles, Poland ranks fifth among the producers of the world; and in the output of rye, potatoes, and sugar beets, she is third. Her three major ports, Gdynia, Gdansk, and Szczecin, handle one half of the maritime traffic on the Baltic Sea.

Remarkably, these achievements have occurred despite the deaths of six million Poles at the hands of the Nazis and the loss of over $60 billion (1945 dollars), or 38 percent, of the national wealth during 1939–1945.

As to the perpetrators of these crimes, the Germans (and I speak here most exclusively of those in the West) have done little

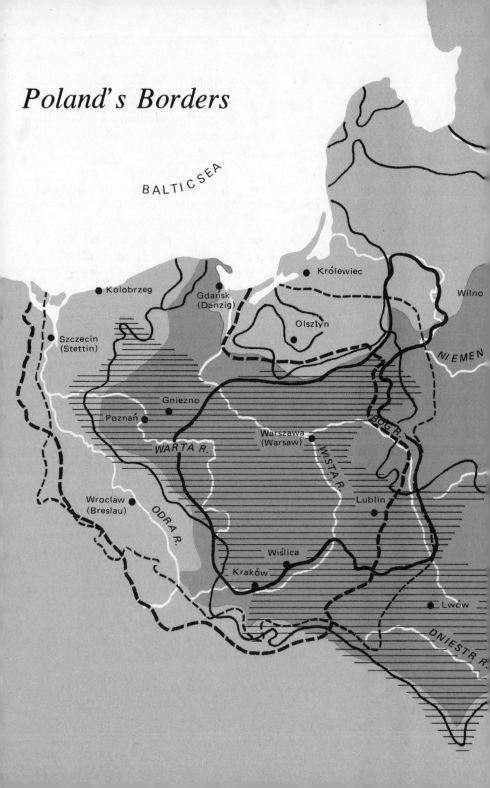

Poland's Borders

BALTIC SEA

Kolobrzeg

Gdańsk
(Danzig)

Królewiec

Wilno

Szczecin
(Stettin)

Olsztyn

NIEMEN

Gniezno

Poznań

WARTA R.

Warszawa
(Warsaw)

WISŁA R.

BUG R.

Wroclaw
(Breslau)

ODRA R.

Lublin

Wiślica

Kraków

Lwów

DNIESTR R.

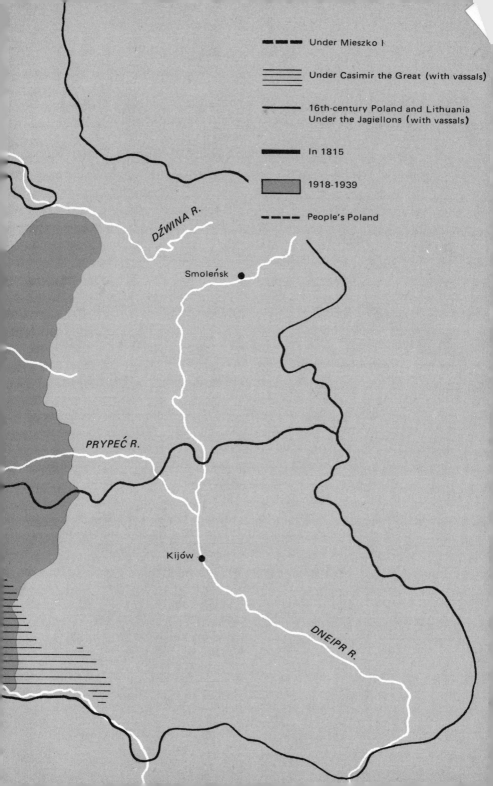

Under Mieszko I

Under Casimir the Great (with vassals)

16th-century Poland and Lithuania
Under the Jagiellons (with vassals)

In 1815

1918-1939

People's Poland

DŹWINA R.

Smoleńsk

PRYPEĆ R.

Kijów

DNEIPR R.

to punish these Nazi criminals, some of whom occupy high official positions there. The nation of Bismarck, Wilhelm, Himmler, Hitler, and the current stunning remilitarization is still not morally rehabilitated. This view is not solely held by Polish, Czech, or Russian political leaders. More importantly, it is the demand of 250 million Slavs who have no intention of permitting the rise of a new Hitler who, ten or fifteen years hence, might again turn their country into one big concentration camp.

The Slav states will never retreat from their firm policy towards Germany, for only by following such a policy can they insure themselves against attempted aggression by a "Fourth Reich." Key to this policy is the preservation of the present Polish western borders. Aside from the defense they afford, these regions, abounding in grain, mines, and factories, are essential to the health of the national economy. Moreover, those Poles who have now made them their home regard the western territories as partial compensation for the horrors they endured during the war. No amount of pressure will force Poland to renounce these regained regions.

Poland's claim to these territories is historically demonstrable and is not open to question. When the country became a nation over 1,000 years ago, her borders extended further west than they do today. The dividing line between Germany and Poland then began at the Baltic Sea and encompassed the left bank of the Oder River and its mouth, at which point was located the town of Szczecin. Also included were Uznam and Wolin islands, the mouth of the Wkra (Ucker) River, including the locality of Pozdawilk (Pasewalk); and the Redowa (Randow) River. Along the Redowa, the border ran towards the south, turning along the Olsza (Welse) River and reaching the Oder River at the town of Swiec. It extended further through the localities of Lesnowola (Freienwalde) and Wrzecien (Wriezen) and southwest at the village of Alt Friedland along the streams of Stobrawa (Stober) and Legnica (Leknitz). It stopped at the Sprewa (Spree) River along which was the locality of Bryland (Friedland), and from here it veered sharply east to reach the mouth of the Lusatian Nisa. This border stood unchanged for more then three hundred years.

Chapter 2

Go back in a moment to my childhood
In a small garden I remember still . . .
By the Wisla an aged cathedral stood,
Grey-spired, upon a high Masovian hill.
When in the silent dusk the old bells had rung
Their benedictions to the fading hour;
While the prone sunset, with a crimson tongue,
Lapped at the purpling river where it flowered.
Over the plains, beside the dark shore there,
The chanting of the forest pine was borne—
A grave, low voice that whispered everywhere;
And in the gloom, the rocks replied forlorn.
Marvel, my heart, as you have done before,
At these old things now blending with the earth!
Although my road marched further into war,
I did not turn aside to know their worth.
Yet dear it is to me, that distant view,
Holding all of time and life's origin and end;
For here it was the speech of learning grew
With which I love and suffer and contend.
Thanks, then, for every word, good people all,
Remembered out of childhood days now grown—
Those humble forest voices I recall
That marked my heart for always as their own.

Wladyslaw Broniewski, a leading Polish poet, who fought rifle in hand during the Second World War, captures in his poetry what I often feel about my country's past.

Yet, much as I would like to convey the richness of her past, I must confine myself to the history that best serves my personal narrative. I therefore begin with the close of the reign of the last king of Slavic blood, Jan Sobieski, when Poland reached her peak in political and cultural splendor. After his death in 1696, affairs in "the republic of the elective kings" went from bad to worse.

The very next king, Frederick Augustus I of Saxony, was elected in 1697 through the support of Prussia and Russia. At his coronation he decided to proclaim himself August II, but the Polish people showed their contempt by calling him "Sas" (Saxon). During his reign, he, together with his ministers and the court, devoted themselves to pleasure-seeking and ignored matters of state. They so gave themselves over to self-indulgence that the people popularized the expression "Eat, drink and be merry with King Sas."

At the instigation of the Prussian King, the Russian tsar, and the Polish nobles, he entangled himself in a war with Sweden in 1701. The war did not go well for Poland, and the nobles lost confidence in Frederick Augustus's leadership. They elected a new king, a Poznan voivode by the name of Stanislaw Leszczynski. But Frederick Augustus refused to relinquish his throne, and so Poland had two kings. This state of affairs so gravely weakened the nation that when the Swedes defeated the Russian army, Augustus was forced to flee to Saxony, leaving the throne to King Stanislaw. Then, when Tsar Peter the Great rallied the Russians to defeat Sweden at the Battle of Poltava, King Stanislaw followed his rival and resigned the throne. August III, the son of August II, was made king. Russia and Prussia had defeated Sweden and in the process two Polish kings had been forced to abdicate their divided throne.

A very tragic period for Poland ensued. Her two neighbors, Russia in the east (where at the tsar's court there were many German advisors) and Prussia in the west, began to interfere actively in the internal affairs of the country. Representatives in the Sejm, bribed by both sides, soon voted for a reduced army. Religious intolerance rose to outrageous heights and ignorant conservatism spread dangerously. The peasant slaves on the estates of the noblemen were permitted no rest and were forced to work even on holidays. Most of the favorable reforms which earnest men had introduced in the Sejm could be nullified, not by majority vote, but by the single vote of any representative who, merely by calling out, "*Liberum veto*," had the power to defeat a resolution. *Liberum veto* had been used long before, but in the eighteenth century its use brought disaster to the entire nation. Now, there were shouts of *liberum veto* from representatives who had been bribed either by the Russian tsar or the German king.

So sordid was the role of the *szlachta* in betraying the interests of Poland that this word for nobleman continues to have an unpleasant and distasteful sound to most Poles. The *szlachta* brought ruin to Poland; nevertheless, they remained proud of their power and proclaimed that "Poland exists only because of disorder." Their demands were the same unreasonable ones made in the nineteenth-century ballad by Adam Mickiewicz, "Pan Twardowski":

> *Now from the sand spin me a whip.*
> *A whip to control my steed.*
> *In yonder woods—goal of my trip*
> *Build me a mansion fine. Indeed!*
> *Its walls from nut meats must be made*
> *And high, as high as Krepak Hills.*
> *The eaves from old men's beards must be laid*
> *From poppy seed the roof and sills.*
> *The size of each nail that you use*
> *Must be an inch thick, three inches long;*
> *Each seed nailed down, because I choose;*
> *With three nails, to make it strong . . .*

Like his Saxon predecessor, King August III knew very little Polish and spoke German exclusively. Also like August II, he devoted all his time to hunting and other diversions, making no attempt to rule. He left the entire administration of the government to his ministers, one of whom, (Count Heinrich von Bruhl, the slyest of the lot, was also a Saxon.)

At this time, the noblemen were divided into two groups: those who already had the ear of the king and his ministers and those who were fighting to gain favor. In the meantime, the peasantry, which constituted 75 percent of the total population, labored day and night for pittance, hardly receiving sufficient relief from their grueling toil to have the energy to devote to their country's problems.

(Small groups of enlightened Polish intellectuals from the ruling class cleverly appealed for the reestablishment of the age-old Polish borders reaching beyond the Nisa and Oder rivers and the ports of the Baltic. But the selfish *szlachta*, who were embroiled in political intrigues and in taking bribes from Poland's neighbors, paid no heed.)

(And so it was that Poland, once a great power in Europe, slowly began to slip to a secondary role. The network of spies and provocateurs within her borders, together with the selfishness of her own nobility, conspired to bring on her downfall.)

As the end of the eighteenth century approached, Poland made her tragic retreat from the Nisa and Oder—and with it came the loss of her independence. For the first time in her 800-year existence, the steadfast policy of encirclement appeared to defeat the Poles.

The Germans had the assistance of the German counselors in the courts of the tsars, who occupied strategic positions in public offices and in the army. A dark and uncertain period of slavery and oppression now awaited the Poles. From the earliest days, their political skills had placed them in the forefront of nations, and for hundreds of years they had managed to resist the brutal *Drang nach Osten*—the German push to the east. On the Elbe, the Nisa, the Oder, and on the Baltic, they had built castles and prosperous towns. Now the Germans seized them all, murdered their people, and even obliterated the ancient Slavic names of their localities. (Berlin itself had once been a Polish settlement, as the German chronicles recorded circa 1244; in the eighteenth century, this very Berlin, now a symbol of Prussian greed, planned the partition of Poland.

The German dynasty of the Hohenzollerns, on the basis of some geographic and economic half-truths as well as family ties, easily persuaded the Austrian Hapsburgs and the Russian Romanoffs that Poland stood in the way of their successful cooperation. These three imperialistic countries, Prussia, Austria, and Russia, which surrounded the shrunken country of Poland, were absolute monarchies and the leading powers of Europe. With such power arrayed against her and with her empty treasury and blind noblemen, Poland was helpless.

The policy of the Romanoffs and Hohenzollerns towards Poland had been created earlier in the century—in 1720—in the Treaty of Potsdam which was designed to eradicate Poland from the map of Europe. Hapsburg Austria, the third party in this understanding, became the junior partner in the trio, while tsarist Russia attempted to induce Poland to accept incorporation into the Russian empire on the basis of common Slavic identity. The Germans, on the other hand, invoked neither blood nor cultural ties. To achieve their aims, they resorted to cold-blooded extermination.

By the end of the eighteenth century, the Germans had received large portions of Polish territory from three successive partitions of Poland. Nevertheless, the Germanization of these lands was not successful. German settlers in the newly acquired territories were unable to assert their cultural supremacy. Therefore, the German government decided systematically to colonize the border regions which would then also be made to serve as military bases. Hence, when the moment was ripe, Germany could move with full force east. Their basic aim was first, *par fas et nefas*, to Germanize Silesia and then the territories located at the middle section of the Oder River and those throughout Pomerania from Szczecin to Krolewiec. This policy of German colonization of Polish lands combined with national uprooting of the Poles had been attempted in the seventeenth and early eighteenth centuries with almost no results. A secret memorandum issued by Frederick II on June 8, 1764, to all his officials reveals the German effort to obliterate the Poles by discouraging the use of the Polish language:

> We earnestly desire that, in those localities and places where only Polish is spoken, the German language should be used as much as possible, so Polish priests have been instructed to perfect themselves in German within a year; Polish teachers are to be removed and their places taken by persons who understand German and who can teach their pupils in German; and furthermore, this aim will not be attained among adults if the children themselves are not inclined to devote themselves with enthusiasm to the good cause. We therefore feel ourselves constrained hereby to ordain and enact that:
>
> 1. No landed estate, under penalty of ten thalers' fine for each breach of this ordinance, shall dare from today's date to receive any one of its subjects of either sex into service in the house or on the farm who does not understand German.
> 2. No girl under the age of eighteen may, from the day of this ordinance, be given permission to marry until she has learned German. *Kaszubs*
> 3. Likewise, no subject of the male sex who has not completed his twentieth year, may likewise be given permission to marry until he has learned German.

This repressive order was followed by other anti-Polish measures. Among them were decrees which provided that all persons of Polish origin be removed from public office; that all businesses belonging to Poles be bought out; that Poles be forbidden to erect new buildings on their own land; and that they be prohibited from wearing their national costume. This program of repression was only the beginning, for when the Poles disregarded all these decrees, Prussia, Austria, and Russia terminated Poland's existence altogether as a separate state in the partitions of 1772, 1793, and 1795. Thus commenced the life-and-death struggle between Poles and Germans, not only on the Nisa and the Oder and in Pomerania, but in the very heart of Poland as well.

Immediately after the first partition of Poland in 1772, when some parts of the country were still unoccupied, a movement towards reform sprang up throughout the country. Progressive leaders urged the building of a modern state based on a broad and intelligent version of national freedom, quite different from the monarchic dictatorships of the neighboring states. The first ministry of education, the Educational Commission, was founded to institute and carry out reforms in the schools. The priest Stanislaw Konarski was the inspiration of these reforms in the elementary and secondary schools. Father Konarski recognized the importance of educating the young: "Our country will be what our children make of it, for some day they will be in charge of it. Children retain the habits and way of thought and life that are inculcated in their childhood. That is why intelligent people know that the welfare of a nation depends on wise and prudent education of the young." Konarski, educator and social worker in a cassock, would later be designated a "red" by twentieth-century reactionaries.

Others who supported social and political reform included the father of the 1791 constitution, Hugo Kollataj, the educator Stanislaw Staszyc, the soldier-author Jozef Wybicki who wrote the national anthem, "Poland is not yet lost," and the lawmaker Andrzej Zamojski. These Polish leaders emulated the progressive ideas of Voltaire, Rousseau, and the French Encyclopedists. Hundreds of writers, educators, manufacturers, and politicians supported reform programs for their dismembered country. The task of these individuals was a formidable one, for their appeal was directed to obstinate noblemen who had lived off the labor of others for hundreds of years. Many of them received incomes of three million *zlotys* or more yearly and funneled the money freely into programs designed to impede social progress and prevent the introduction of reforms.

But under the influence of social reformers, a Sejm was assembled in 1788 in truncated Poland to deliberate on civic improvements and enact laws in the political and social spheres. The timing of the Sejm was most opportune, for Russia was then occupied in a war with Turkey and the German king was attempting to form an alliance with Poland against Russia. The Sejm deliberated for four years, during which time liberal French thought

infiltrated Poland. In Paris, the first democratic parliament, known
as the General Assembly, was established, and very shortly thereafter, the French king, Louis XVI, ceased to be called the "Lord's
Annointed" and became "Citizen Louis Capet."

In Polish towns, political clubs patterned on the French were
formed among the poor. The lesser nobles in the villages now
began to back wide social reforms in the country rather than the
millionaire counts and princes. Revolts broke out among the
poverty-stricken and oppressed peasants. The great educator,
sociologist, and reformer Stanislaw Staszyc demanded that the
four-year-old Sejm abolish serfdom, divide the land among the
peasants, and grant the same rights to the townspeople as the
noblemen enjoyed. He also advocated the establishment of a
hereditary throne, the expansion of the army to 100,000 men, and
the abolition of the pernicious *liberum veto*.

Hugo Kollataj went much further: he demanded peasant representatives in the Sejm and the restoration to Poland of Silesia, a
region rich in coal and iron which was then controlled by Prussia.
Franciszek Jezierski, the crusading writer, distributed fiery pam-
phlets throughout the country which called upon the peasants, the
lesser noblemen, and the townspeople to appeal to the then ruling
Polish king, Stanislaw August Poniatowski, for support of reform
programs and progressive measures. They were also asked to
pledge their aid in the struggle against the Germans.

In this atmosphere the Constitution of the Third of May was
born in 1791 and was passed by the Sejm in Warsaw. It was a very
enlightened document for that time. It strengthened the power of
the king and abolished the *liberum veto*, stating that any bill passed
by a majority vote in the Sejm would be considered valid. All bills
were to be submitted to the Sejm, which was to assemble regularly
every two years. The rights of the townspeople were made equal to
those of the noblemen, but the peasant was refused comparable
freedom. From that time on, however, all disputes arising between
the peasants and nobles were to be settled by the state court;
theoretically, a peasant could now free himself from serfdom by
paying rent for his land.

While the constitution provided that the peasant was no

longer the exclusive property of the noblemen on whose estate he lived, its failure to grant him equal constitutional rights was most unjust since the peasants formed the majority of the population. As difficult times loomed ahead for Poland, the government should have had the complete support of the peasants, the backbone of the nation. The state should have made at least a pretense of granting them independence in order to gain their support in the struggle for a better position for Poland in Europe.

Yet, even the few reforms that were passed, weak and restricted as they were, were deemed excessive by the powerful and wealthy magnates such as Szczesny Potocki, Ksawery Branicki, and Seweryn Rzewuski, who mortgaged themselves to the Russians and Germans. A few days after the constitution was enacted, they formed a conspiracy in the town of Targowica in the Ukraine and sought the help of the Russian army. Against these treacherous enemies of the constitution, the state authority dispatched an army of 30,000 soldiers under the leadership of the king's nephew, Jozef Poniatowski, and two generals, Tadeusz Kosciuszko and Jozef Zajaczek. Kosciuszko became known as the "Hero of Two Continents" for his part in the United States' War of Independence and in his own country's fight for freedom from oppression. He had a broader conception of liberty than most of his contemporaries. For his role in the American struggle he was made an honorary citizen of the United States by the Congress in 1783.

The battle was an unequal one, with King Stanislaw himself defecting to the enemy army. The patriots were defeated, and, as a result, Russia and Prussia partitioned Poland a second time in 1793. The new Polish constitution was annulled.

In the summer of 1794, another uprising broke out against the enemy invaders. The "Kosciuszko Insurrection," as it was called, was put down in spite of the heroism of thousands of peasants led by Wojciech Bartosz. In 1795, a third, and, this time, complete partition of Poland took place. Russia, Prussia, and Austria seized the remaining Polish territory, including Gdansk, Warsaw, Cracow, Lublin, and other large cities. Poland now ceased to exist as a separate state. The Poles' struggle for freedom, however, did not come to an end.

After the partitions, life was unbearable under the rule of Prussia and Austria for the Poles in the territories extending to the Niemen, Bug, and Zbrucz rivers. The invaders began the so-called third step in colonization, organized and directed completely by their government agencies. The government promised the peasants of western and southern Prussia that they would be granted freedom from taxes and military service for a two-year period and that they would be allotted larger farms if they agreed to migrate. Those who refused were transplanted by force across the Nisa and the Oder and to Eastern Pomerania. Soldiers under official orders would encircle a German village and forcibly remove the inhabitants and their belongings to Polish villages in Silesia or near the Baltic; the Poles who had lived in these areas were deported to localities near the Vistula. More often, however, German peasants and townsmen voluntarily left for the Polish territories, encouraged by their government's offer of better working conditions, bigger farms, and opportunities to loot the Polish population. In a very short time, 150,000 new colonists were settled in the province of Brandenburg; 67,000 at the mouth of the Oder; 26,500 in the towns of Kolobrzeg, Slupsk, and Bytom; 219,000 on the banks of the Warta and Notec rivers; 11,000 in the town of Grudziadz and vicinity; 2,000 in Chelmno; and 2,500 in Plock and vicinity. This Germanization of Poland was to continue throughout the nineteenth century.

There was new hope for Poland when the French came in 1806. When Napoleon made peace with Russia in the city of Tylza on the Niemen River in 1807, he had an opportunity to create an independent Poland. The Poles had helped him vanquish the Austrian, Russian, and Prussian armies; in all some 43,000 Poles died while in Napoleon's service. But in return for their loyalty and sacrifices, he gave them a part of central Poland, the Grand Duchy of Warsaw, which had a population of only 2.5 million.

With Napoleon's final defeat and exile in 1815, representatives of England, Austria, Prussia, Russia, Spain, Sweden, Portugal, and France assembled in Vienna to deliberate the future of Europe. In the course of the Congress of Vienna, Russia offered to found a Polish state similar to Napoleon's Grand Duchy of War-

saw. Part of the Grand Duchy was to be known as the Congres-
sional Kingdom of Poland, and the governing king would be
known as the "holy" Russian tsar. The other part became known
as the Grand Duchy of Posen and was placed under Prussian rule.
Thus, the three foreign occupying powers had created a fictitiously
independent Poland, and each had succeeded in destroying the
country economically and culturally, systematically setting one
section of the Polish people against the other and class against
class.

In the 1820s, Polish patriots began to organize secret societies
in preparation for an armed uprising against the hated occupying
powers. These secret groups soon began to spread. University
students, intellectuals, the middle class of the towns, and even the
workers were joining ranks. Only the peasants took no active part.
They had good reason for not joining, for they had had no freedom
during Poland's independence and, consequently, after Poland
lost her sovereignty, they had neither gained nor lost.

One of the societies was the *Filareci*, which was formed in
the city of Wilno. Its motto was "Motherland, Knowledge and
Virtue." One of its leading members was Adam Mickiewicz, at
this time a young writer. His poems helped inspire the people to
resist the foreign rulers. In his "Ode to Youth," Mickiewicz cried
out:

> *Together, young friends;*
> *Happiness for all is everyone's goal.*

In this poem, which became a bible for Polish youth, he
condemned selfishness and extolled the power of cooperation in
promoting the interests of the whole of society.

During this period of subjugation in the first quarter of the
nineteenth century, a liberal Masonic organization was reborn,
with lodges established throughout the country and headquarters
set in Warsaw. Belonging to these secret Masonic lodges were
prominent people from the worlds of literature, science, politics,
and the army—men like Major Walerian Lukasinski, Stanislaw
Staszyc, Hugo Kollataj, and Joachim Lelewel. The Masons were

active and worked unceasingly to unite the nation in readiness for the moment of liberation.

The liberal spirit in Poland grew stronger after 1830, influenced by the revolutions that were occurring in much of Europe. In this year, the Belgians rose up against their Dutch rulers and the French against the ruling Bourbon family. A popular uprising of the Poles against the occupying powers erupted in January 1831, but those who had organized it had failed to attract the broad masses of the peasantry. The insurrection was completely suppressed by the Russians, and some of the best Polish youths were killed. Mickiewicz described the grisly destruction wrought by the Tsar's armies:

> . . . *A corpse, whose feet*
> *Are tangled in the winding sheet,*
> *A struck match with a sulphur smell*
> *From the sooty tinderbox of hell.*
> *Wearing glasses in skull eye-bones*
> *Of golden plate, two glowing stones;*
> *And in each rounded throne there sits*
> *Satan-like, an evil sprite*
> *Turning endless handsprings on a spit.*
> *The corpse, with chattering teeth, must jump;*
> *From knuckles to loose knuckles, as sieves,*
> *He drops through silver, melted lumps;*
> *Groaning because he cannot live.*
>
> *The tsar moves like the sun; the loyal armies*
> *Revolve like the planets on the celestial stage.*
> *The tsar unleashes his auxiliaries*
> *Like packs of hounds, or sparrows from a cage;*
> *Madly they shout commands, madly they race,*
> *Official voices barking every place;*
> *The bass drums growl, musicians whisper and whine.*
> *Now anchor-cable-wise the infantry*
> *Unwinds and snaps out like a whip. . . .*

The Germans had pledged to help the Russians, but held back as long as possible, reasoning that a Russia weakened by war would be easier to deal with. Hence, they limited their assistance to tracking down insurrectionists who had escaped into their territories. After the uprising was quelled, the Polish language was banned altogether from schools, churches, administrative bodies, and the judiciary. German prisons were jammed with almost 50,000 Polish political prisoners. In 1833, the Germans spent one million *talars* in gold in the struggle against the rightful owners of the land east of the Oder River.

Despite further oppression, the Polish people did not give up their struggle for national liberation. Thousands of soldiers, writers, and scientists escaped from the German and Russian terror in Poland and went to France, Switzerland, or Italy, where they began to organize for future independence. Among the emigrés were three of Poland's greatest poets: Adam Mickiewicz, Juliusz Slowacki, and Zygmunt Krasinki.

Another Polish artist who went into exile at this time was Fryderyk Chopin. During all his years abroad, he made many attempts to return to Poland to fight the oppressors, but his friends, knowing that he had tuberculosis, prevented his going back. Though he anguished over his physical inability to aid his country, the music he composed became the monument of his love and sorrow for his homeland. His "Etude in C Minor," known as the "Revolutionary Etude," contains his impassioned cry for "Liberty, Equality, Fraternity" and his burning love for his comrades who struggled for Poland's freedom.

The year 1848 was the "People's Spring" in Europe, with revolutions against the monarchical dictatorships breaking out in Paris, Berlin, Vienna, and Budapest. Among the shouts of the insurgent, struggling masses, there were also voices calling for the freedom of Poland. As a result of these uprisings, the despotic monarchs were forced to grant constitutions to their people. France became a republic. Great numbers of Polish emigrés rushed home to help the revolutionists. In Poland, a secret government was formed, and a temporary underground army of 10,000 men was organized under the command of General Ludwik

Mieroslawski. But the powerful Germans, Russians, and Austrians crushed all of these Polish revolts, one after the other. The Polish conservatives helped the usurpers by appealing to the people to accept their fate and live under a peace imposed by foreign rulers.

The leaders of the conservatives, Aleksander Wielopolski, Tytus Dzialynski, and Professor Antoni Helcel from Cracow, played for time. They proposed a gradual reorganization of the economic life of the country, raising its standard of living and building public schools for the education of the masses. Then, in a hundred years or so, they argued, the nation would be able to fight and to conquer the enemy. But the Polish democrats went straight to the people and set to work to organize and prepare them for immediate armed struggle.

While all of these strategies were being proposed, the people were suffering under a double oppression. In the Prussian sector, the Poles were driven off their farms and German colonists were settled in their place. Polish school and church buildings were used as arsenals, army barracks, or German cultural institutions. In the Russian sector, a similar situation prevailed. The new Tsar Alexander II, upon his arrival in Warsaw in 1862, announced: "Give up your dreams of freedom. All revolts will be promptly put down."

Only in the Austrian part of Poland were conditions a little better for the people. In 1859, the Hapsburg Emperor of Austria-Hungary, after he had lost the war with France and Italy, restored some civil liberties and allowed parliament to assemble in his empire.

In 1862 at the instigation of the Polish traitor, Margrave Wielopolski, the Russian tsar drew up a plan for forcing all young Polish men into the Russian army. The secret Polish government discovered the plan and set January 22, 1863, as the day for an uprising. They also issued a manifesto declaring the abolition of serfdom. The document began as follows: "All of Poland's sons, regardless of race or religion, class or national origin, are hereby declared free and equal citizens! Join the ranks of the patriots and fight for the independence of your country!"

Conflict flared up in every part of Poland. The reverberations of this new insurrection echoed throughout the democratic world, reaching as far as America, which at that time was occupied with her own civil war. U.S. Secretary of State William Seward said of the Poles that they were "a gallant nation whose wrongs, whose misfortunes, and whose valor have so deeply excited universal sympathy."

The Germans and Russians sent out more than 200,000 of their best soldiers against the Polish revolutionaries. Because the insurrectionists were unable to organize a regular army, they fought as partisans, attacking their enemy from ambush in the forests and mountains. But at times they also came out into the open and fought, as when General Marian Langiewicz and his detachment engaged part of the Russian army in battle and won.

In addition to men of many different nationalities—Poles, Jews, Ukrainians, Byelorussians, Lithuanians—many women actively participated in the courageous struggle. Not only did these women take actual part in battle, but they also supplied false passports, carried money, hid important documents, and engaged in other crucial missions. Two Jewish sisters by the name of Hierch performed so many brave deeds that their names and exploits became known to everyone. The Russian government promised a reward of a thousand *rubles* to anyone who would divulge the whereabouts of another courageous woman, Jadwiga Wolska. Henryka Pustowojt served as adjutant to General Langiewicz. A French teacher, Maria A. Lix, became a legendary figure for her bravery when the commander of her regiment was killed on the battlefield and she took over command. An enemy bullet ripped into her head and almost killed her. Wounded, she was taken prisoner. While being dragged away, half alive, to be questioned, she managed to escape into the woods and rejoin her own people.

Without question, however, the bravest of them all was Wiktoria Jankiewicz. During the battle near Uniejow in 1863, her regiment was besieged by an overwhelming force of Germans. Seeing no hope for the patriots, she explained the desperate situation to them and demonstrated that the only way out was by way of

the bridge which spanned the Warta River. When the insurrectionists finally crossed over, she ignited some barrels filled with
gunpowder that blew up the bridge just as the Germans were
crossing.

In spite of the heroism of the women and the defiant spirit of
the ill-clad, poorly equipped partisans and soldiers of different
nationalities, the insurrection was again cruelly suppressed.

Romuald Traugutt, the head of the Polish national government, was captured by the Russians and with four of his fellow
countrymen was sent to the gallows in the Warsaw citadel on
August 5, 1864. In their reprisals the German and Russian governments persecuted the Poles unmercifully. Thousands were
condemned to forced labor in the coal mines or were sentenced to
the gallows. Those who had some resources went into exile
abroad. Again, all of Europe sympathized with the Polish refugees
and gave them welcome. Hundreds journeyed to America where
they worked on farms and in factories, finding bread and freedom
in their new country. In time, more and more immigrants came to
this land where Pulaski and Kosciuszko had won a permanent
place in American history.

Although the insurrection of 1863 was a failure, the people of
Poland held on to their hope of regaining independence and of
making a reality of the People's Spring. With passionate defiance
and unshakable obstinacy, they continued to prepare to challenge
the tyrants and once and for all drive out the oppressors. Having
learned from their experience in previous uprisings, the intellectuals sought to gain the support of the peasants. They went to them
directly, lectured them, and discussed mutual problems on a level
of equality.

National feeling grew despite oppression. Austria, Russia
and Prussia tried in vain to suppress everything Polish. But the
whole nation, all classes now included, engaged in a quiet, determined struggle, working to rebuild their country spirtually and
materially. Despite many setbacks, progress was made, and the
people maintained their faith in ultimate freedom. Masses of the
common people were learning the role they were to play in the
eventual liberation of their country.

In 1885, as a result of ever growing rivalry between the imperialism of Germany and Russia, Bismarck instituted even sharper repressive measures against the Poles. His rationale was that the Poles and Russians would eventually come to a mutual understanding and that both would thereupon turn against Germany. In March of that year, 50,000 Poles received orders to leave Poland.

The period of the *Kulturkampf*, the struggle led by Bismarck against the patriotic Polish clergy in the territories on the Nisa and Oder rivers, was followed by the period of the *HaKaTa* (a name taken from the initials of the last names of the three German organizers of this movement, Hansemann, Kennemann, and Tiedemann), a violent struggle against the Polish masses, especially the peasantry. None of the nefarious measures devised by the Germans succeeded in moving the peasants from their land. In one year alone, the enemy spent a hundred million marks on this struggle.

The determination of the peasants to hold on to their lands and the faith they had in eventually ousting the enemy are illustrated in the following anecdote: In the spring of 1897, in the village of Jawory, a town near Bolkow in Silesia, the father of Jan Bolkowicz, Mieczyslaw, was ousted from his farm. He built himself a shed on the edge of the public road to which he moved his wife and seven children. From here he could view his house and the fields that he had sown with his own hands the past autumn and which now were occupied by Karl Krantz from western Germany. But the stubborn Pole could do nothing about it; for against him were arrayed not only Krantz, who had stolen his house and land, but the whole apparatus of German law that had brought him here. In order to make a living, Bolkowicz worked on the community road, and, from afar, kept an eye on his stolen property. He would say to his comrades-in-misery, pointing to the road he was working on, "Don't worry, some fine day the Fritzes and Krantzes will be running away down this very road, running back to Berlin; and, in spite of everything, the Poles will get their land back. They'll come back to Silesia, to Lubusz and Pomerania, back to their own land, their own soil. Only have courage, brothers, have patience!"

Chapter 3

our youth they have uptorn
from earths delight
dragging them by their hearts
                              roots
                              with no more
                              than a single
                              grain
                              of patriotic
                              dynamite
dark judases
of nations

now
brains and feet
keep pace   identical divisions
ignite
      europe   americas
                asia
advance in joy newfangled to glory
with rotted skulls dangled
from bayonets
                jangle your hymns
with nationalistic faces
while
their
graces
tiptoe traders in ideals
                        kicking
                        their own posteriors
                        with their heels
                        order
                        us hanged
                        as a new
            laudation
                      of the dictators by the strangled

The First World War, which began on July 28, 1914, was a contest between the leading European governments for the control of Europe and the world. All the fine-sounding slogans generated during the war, such as "the rights of small nations" and "making the world safe for democracy," were propaganda designed to mask the imperialistic ambitions of the great powers. The comparatively recent revelation that the *Lusitania* secretly carried large supplies of arms destined for English use against Germany confirms this fact. Of course, none of the 1,195 passengers who died from the German torpedoing were aware of the *Lusitania's* false bottom. And neither were the American people who were subjected to a barrage of "hate the Hun" propaganda and other forms of governmental repression.

Since the Central Powers and the Allies were out to get for themselves as large a share as possible of the natural resources, means of production, and markets of the world as they could, all manner of duplicity was permissible. In order to maintain their position of power, the ruling classes had to resort to fomenting national rivalries and ethnic divisions, for class divisions were great and working class political consciousness was high. The manufacturers of arms and ammunition did their part in keeping the world situation inflamed, for, with magnificient impartiality, they sold to both sides.

When the war was over and ten million people had been sent to their graves, the victorious Allies decided that Germany's continued aggressions could be best directed eastwards. Hence, in their deliberations over the border problem between Germany and Poland in the Treaty of Versailles, the victorious powers ignored Poland's claims for the restoration of her rightful borders on the Nisa, Oder, and the Baltic. They had two reasons: first, German policy-makers were willing to play up to the business interests of the three Allied powers, England, France, and the United States, offering to become the tool of the financial cartels in exchange for aid in rebuilding German industry; second, revolution had broken out in Russia in 1917, and, under the leadership of Lenin, had given birth to the Soviet Republic. To choke off this "Bolshevik epidemic," the Allies worked for a strong Germany and a meek, obedient Poland which would serve as a bulwark to "stop Bolshevism."

There was one Allied leader, however—President Woodrow Wilson—who advocated Poland's political independence. Wilson has been portrayed alternately as a schemer and a dreamer. His ideal of a League of Nations and international cooperation on American terms was ridiculed not only by hardheaded American businessmen who were more interested in sales than in the responsibilities of international leadership, but also by principled anti-imperialists like Senators William Borah, George Norris, and Robert LaFollette. Nationalist leaders abroad also opposed his conception of world order. It was in his speech before the U.S. Congress on January 8, 1918, that Wilson proposed freedom for Poland: "An independent Polish state should be erected which should include the territories inhabited by an indisputably Polish population, which should be assured of a free and secure access to the sea, and whose political and economic independence and territorial integrity should be guaranteed by international covenant."

This statement was the distillation of discussions held as far back as the autumn of 1915 between Wilson and the Polish pianist and patriot Paderewski, who reaffirmed the President's desire to readmit Poland into the family of independent nations. But at Versailles in 1919, the businessmen won and Wilson lost. As a result, Poland underwent worse mutilation in the west from the Versailles Treaty than from the Congress of Vienna in 1815.

The Poles had fought in the First World War on every front and sector in the hopes of ultimately regaining their rightful borders on the Oder and Nisa. Now that dream vanished. According to the terms of the Treaty of Versailles, Poland won some land in Upper Silesia and was granted a 140-kilometer coastline on the Baltic Sea. But the grant of Upper Silesia would prove to be only temporary, and Gdansk, the chief port on this coastline, effectively remained in German hands. East Prussia, the plague spot of German generals and imperialists, also remained with the Germans. Clearly, the Polish people were betrayed. In August, 1919, a bloody Polish uprising broke out in Lower Silesia and in the part of Upper Silesia that was not yielded to Poland. It was crushed by German troops, who suffered heavy casualties of their own.

After the First World War, England refused to recognize the rights of Poland to the western territories. But even some German historians did not deny these rights. In 1926, Joseph Pfitzner wrote:

> The territory of Silesia had had no existence as yet as a political concept, but the territory on the middle Oder did come to be considered, not only geographically but also politically, a Polish creation, with its center of gravity in the areas between the middle Oder and the Vistula. Boleslaw the Brave reached the territories on the left bank of the Oder River up to Karkonosze, which became his by all natural and national rights, and incorporated them in full into the Polish realm, which was born and reached maturity during his reign. (*Besiedlungs- Verfassungs- und Vervaltungsgeschichte des Breslauer Bistumslandes,* I, Reichenberg, 1926)

Nevertheless, at Versailles Poland not only lost her territories in the west, but her access to the sea was reduced to an area called the "Corridor"—an isolated strip of land extending through predominantly Polish Pomerania, which, after the war, was handed over to Germany. Two American professors, Charles H. Haskins and Robert H. Lord, advisers to the Department of State during the peace conference, emphasized Poland's territorial needs: "Poland needs access to the sea; but it was not solely because she needs it that she obtained it. The Peace Conference probably would not have satisfied this desire if ethnical reasons had not authorized it to do so. The Conference did not invent the 'Corridor,' it existed already, and it is clearly inscribed on all honestly compiled linguistical maps." (*Some Problems of the Peace Conference,* Cambridge, 1920)

A former English Undersecretary of Foreign Affairs, Hugh Dalton, also confirmed Poland's rights to an outlet to the sea: "The so-called 'Corridor' is inhabited by an indisputably Polish population . . . . On grounds of nationality, the case of Poland retaining the 'Corridor' is very strong already, and will grow with every year that passes. (*Towards the Peace of Nations,* London, 1928)

The young Polish Republic that rose from the ashes of national extinction in November 1918 faced grave economic and political problems. At this favorable historical moment, most Poles wanted the problem of the western boundary settled once and for all. Specifically, they wanted the restoration of the Nisa and Oder rivers and an outlet to the Baltic. Unfortunately, however, the will of the majority was of little consequence, for a small group of Russophobe adventurers had power over Poland's foreign policy. Thus, rather than fight for the western territory, they directed their military lust toward aggression on Poland's eastern borders.

Fortified by the warmest blessings of France and England and by the most modern weapons and most skilled military advisers, an army was raised in Poland to invade the Ukraine. The purpose was an international attempt to overthrow the Bolshevik regime. The leader of the Polish army, General Jozef Pilsudski, succeeded in reaching the gates of Kiev, but was forced back to the gates of Warsaw. Contributing to the defeat were the vast Ukrainian steppes that historically had swallowed even the biggest armies, plus the determined stand of the Ukrainians.

Immediately upon the return of Pilsudski's exhausted, weakened army, the Allied Council on July 28, 1920, decreed that the extensive Polish population on the Czech-Polish border in the region known as Cieszyn-Silesia be incorporated into the new country of Czechoslovakia. At the same time, Germany was making plans to overrun all of Silesia and the west-central parts of Poland. In anticipation of this new German aggression, the Second Silesian Insurrection of peasants and workers broke out on August 20, 1920. Poland, only recently freed from more than a century of national enslavement and still weakened by world war, was further exhausted by the two Silesian campaigns and by her role in the international invasion of the Soviet Union.

At this time, Lloyd George and his counselors ordered a plebiscite to be held in Upper Silesia to demonstrate that even this part of the great industrial region rightfully belonged to Germany. The plebiscite took place on March 20, 1921, under the supervision of the Allies hostile to the Polish cause. The German military police and the entire German bureaucratic apparatus mobilized to insure victory. The results were 707,000 votes in favor of joining the Reich and only 479,000 for Poland. The results could easily have been foretold, for 300,000 Germans were imported into Upper Silesia from central Germany very shortly before the voting.

As a result of the phony plebiscite, the Third Silesian Insurrection erupted on May 2, 1921. In his work, *Kampf um Annaberg* (Berlin, 1930), Arthur Mohaupt, a German writer and a participant in the struggle for Silesian control, states that England supplied the Germans with guns and ammunition. Other writers, such as General Karl Hoefer in *Oberschlesien in der Aufstandszeit* (Berlin, 1931), and Captain Manfred Killinger, in *Kampf um Oberschlesien* (Hamburg, 1932), clearly point out that there were more Poles than Germans in Upper Silesia. But Lloyd George chose to aid the suppression of the Polish population in these regions. Thus, the Poles had to rely on their own resources and on Wojciech Korfanty, one of the leaders of the Second Silesian Insurrection. Even though the Germans had the best arms England could supply, the Poles challenged the enemy bravely. Nevertheless, the Germans and English crushed the Third Silesian Insurrection, and this age-old Polish territory was formally divided into two parts on October 20, 1921, by the Council of Ambassadors, a body established by the Allies to sanctify injustice. The very same year dishonesty was repeated in East Prussia where another "Western-style" plebiscite yielded similar results.

The secret of German success was not a complex one. As already noted, the German politicians were skillful in dealing with the Allies, and the Allies feared the Soviet Union. The third reason for Berlin's successes, and no less important, was England's fear of a powerful France on the continent. To counteract the threatened hegemony of France in Europe, England needed a strong Germany. England's fears proved futile, for France, weakened by war, had no leadership left. Even so, the English policy-makers sought to bolster Germany's material build-up and encourage her imperialistic ambitions. Adding to England's fears was the fact that Soviet Russia had failed to fall apart as predicted.

In 1918, Berlin found it politically expedient to get rid of the
Hohenzollern, Kaiser Wilhelm, but left his generals in place. With
the help of a new leader and of the coal and iron riches from the
ill-gotten mines of Silesia, they were left free to plot yet another
Drang nach Osten.

Immediately after the Versailles Treaty was signed, German
industrialists invested capital in rebuilding their heavy industry.
They were assisted by English and U.S. bankers and by any
financiers, politicians, adventurers, and speculators who saw easy
money in Germany's plans to expand eastward. As a preliminary
move in their plans, Berlin's most important task was the Germanization of over a million Poles who were then living within the
borders of the Reich. The German government pressed for the
complete eradication of all things Polish in the acquired territories,
from Polish historical and cultural symbols to the names of the
cities, towns, and villages. The Germans also initiated an efficient
network of spies on Polish territory.

The one man in Poland who appeared able to capture public
support to meet the German threats to internal security in the 1920s
was Jozef Pilsudski. So far though, Pilsudski had made his military mark fighting Russians rather than Germans. Nevertheless,
the left at first backed him, for he did not seem to have the support
of the *szlachta* or big-business elements. Moreover, Pilsudski had
once been associated with the Socialist Party. Thus, the left further
confused his brash military conduct with revolutionary fervor. The
right opposed him, fearing the concentration of political power in
one man rather than the traditional oligarchy. In 1926, using troops
personally loyal to him, Pilsudski pressured the existing government into resigning. For the last nine years of his life, he delighted
the right and angered the left by his policies of preserving the status
quo. He did nothing to narrow the gap between rich and poor. By
the time he died in 1935, the right supported him, while the left
opposed him.

His spiritual successor, Colonel Jozef Beck, was less tact-
ful, more dictatorial than Pilsudski and lacked his charisma.
The Polish economy was in such decline that the regime could
not have been liberalized without sacrificing the power of the

szlachta and domestic and foreign big-business interests. During the entire interwar period, productivity reached pre-World-War-I levels in only one year—1929. With the onset of the Great Depression, the Polish economy collapsed altogether. It was not restored until after the Second World War when it was developed through socialism.

Tragically, the Depression led to the unleashing of the Nazi terror throughout Europe. The Poles in German territories were subjected to many cruelties. The Nazis broke into Polish homes, kidnapped the children, and sent them into the depths of the Reich for Germanization. Older folk were given the alternative of packing and moving east at once or swearing allegiance to Adolf Hitler and working on German *latifundia*. Able-bodied men were impressed into the army, despite Section 173 of the Treaty of Versailles which clearly stated: "There will be no forced military service in Germany. The army can only receive those who enter it as volunteers."

German scientists and writers justified the Nazi crimes on the basis of some so-called facts from history. More often than not, these "facts" were based on myths. One of these myths had Germanic tribes living in Poland's western territories from time immemorial, but it had no solid historical evidence. Germans created their own facts with the sword.

It would be well to pause a moment here to read what Friedrich Nietzsche had to say about the German national character. The Nazis used Nietzsche's philosophy freely to justify their crimes, and Hitler regarded him as official philosopher of the Third Reich.

German historians are political jokers who have not only destroyed the evolution and refinement of culture but also have destroyed the power of observation. According to them, before one can decide what is valuable and what is not valuable *in historicis*, one has first to be a "German" and to have "race." "Germanism" is an argument, "German first and foremost," a principle; Germans are "the moral order of the world" in history. When I read such statements, I feel

eager, I even consider it my duty to tell the Germans everything of which they are guilty. They are guilty of all the
important crimes of four centuries. The reason remains the
same, their intense cowardice in the face of reality, which at
the same time is cowardice before truth, wherein their
"idealism" is transformed to an instinctive yearning for
unreality. Germans have deprived Europe of its meaning and
its reason, which it can never hope to regain!

Naturally, the above analysis of the German character by the
author of *Thus Spoke Zarathustra* and *Man and Superman* was not
included in the complete Nazi edition of his works. Instead, Dr.
Goebbels's Ministry of Propaganda popularized among the German masses a more suitable author, namely, Herr Blunck, who, in
his book *Koenig Gersereich* (a novel on the Vandals' conquest of
Rome which attained great popularity during the Nazi era) tried to
prove that vandalism was neither barbaric nor reprehensible. He
also claimed that the German nation should take pride in its Vandal
ancestry because the Vandals were a unique people who had
demonstrated an excellent synchronization of conquest with the
sentiments of modern-day Germanic morality. Once conquest was
achieved and governing was begun, German morality would express novel concepts of law and order, never before attempted by
any other civilization.
     Unfortunately for Poland, Jozef Beck did not recognize the
Nazi peril until too late. Hitler saw that the Western capitalist
powers were willing to sacrifice Slavs, Jews, and Gypsies in order
to maintain power in their own countries. He read the Western
press. He listened to the speeches of Western leaders. He knew
that a German march to the East would meet with no military
resistance from the West. He was right. And even in the West,
exceptions like Spain would be made. Hitler's military madness
was to believe that he could attack East and West simultaneously.
     The U.S.S.R. was fully aware of Hitler's intentions. She
knew war was inevitable, just as clearly as Herman Hesse did
when he wrote *Steppenwolf* in 1929. So the Soviets tried very hard
in the 1930s to make the Western powers aware that Hitler would

not be content with the Soviet Union alone but would want the whole world to be Germany's slave.

For this reason, she had joined the League of Nations in 1934, signed a mutual assistance pact with France in 1935 and another with Czechoslovakia, and sent military aid to the beleaguered defenders of the Spanish republic against the onslaughts of Franco and Hitler. When Hitler marched into Prague on March 15, 1939, the Soviet foreign minister Litvinov sharply attacked this move.

In contrast was England's Prime Minister Chamberlain whose reaction was mild. Public outcry against the latest manifestation of Chamberlain's appeasement of Hitler, backed by opinion polls that showed that 85 percent of the English people were in favor of an Anglo-Soviet alliance, forced him two weeks later to a paper guarantee that England would give Poland military support if she were attacked. One month later, the U.S.S.R. proposed a ten-year Anglo-French-Soviet alliance which would include Rumania and Poland. England turned down the Soviet offer, and in May Molotov replaced Litvinov.

Molotov was as staunchly anti-Nazi as Litvinov had been, but he was highly critical of the English and French governments' repeated refusals to enter into a military alliance with the Soviet Union. He realized that Hitler, Mussolini, and Japanese militarists had risen to power on the backs of their industrialists who wanted desperately to contain the socialist threats to their own power within their own countries. In his attack on Germany in his speech of May 31, Molotov proclaimed that the fascist powers were using this excuse as a pretext to conquer the world, while England, France, and the United States sat on the sidelines hoping that the Axis powers would somehow vent all their wrath on the Soviet Union.

But this was not to be the case, as Hitler, the kingpin of the most historically vile of all alliances, was as doubledealing as he was bloodthirsty. On August 21, Molotov was given the opportunity to educate the entire world on this point by signing the Moscow-Nazi Pact, but not before he had made one last frustrating—and vain—effort to work out a military pact with England and France. The American historian Gabriel Kolko has noted that the pact was signed "only after it appeared likely that Britain preferred a Nazi-Soviet war as the lesser evil."

Meanwhile, in Poland Colonel Beck sought to maintain himself in power in the face of economic adversity by blaming the minority population of the country, which comprised 30 percent of her people, for Poland's problems. He played upon nationalist divisions by encouraging anti-Semitism, and he aroused nationalist pride by attacking the Czechs for mistreating Poles in the western sector of Cieszyn-Silesia, the region unilaterally yielded to Czechoslovakia by the Allies in 1920. After Hitler occupied Czechoslovakia in 1938, Beck occupied Cieszyn-Silesia. Poland and Germany were rendered moral equals in the Anglo-French press. Nonetheless, the British and the French continued to placate, and even favor, fascist Germany as a counterweight to Soviet communism.

Other public acts which won Beck friends among the fascists in the 1930s were his equivocation on Mussolini's rape of Ethiopia, his official recognition of the Japanese puppet state of Manchukuo in China, and his prosecution of Poles who fought Franco and Hitler in Spain. Most serious of all was his refusal to enter into Franco-Soviet and Soviet-Czech alliances to stop fascism.

Beck's foreign policy was a disaster for Poland. On September 1, 1939, Hitler surprised the Polish people with a *blitzkrieg* that killed hundreds of thousands. What remained of Beck's government fled to London and set up a government-in-exile, while a Polish army of some 75,000 was sequestered in the Soviet Union. The position of the Poles in London reveals why the Soviet Union was hostile to the London government and why Churchill and Roosevelt also found the Poles impossible to deal with. Throughout the entire conflict, during which twenty million Russians died fighting fascism, the London Poles argued that they would fight either against the Russians or against the Germans only if their participation hurt the Russians. To a Russia that in one generation had twice seen Eastern and Central Europe made into a hostile springboard for German aggression, this position was obviously unacceptable.

Hitler formally invaded the Soviet Union on June 20, 1941. For the next two years the world situation seemed as bleak as it had been since civilization began. Fortunately, the Allies knew in advance of Hitler's commands to his generals in the field. With the help of a Polish mechanic who had memorized its workings, and Polish technicians and engineers who were able to reconstruct it, the key German coding machine used for transmitting most communications within the German high command was made available to English intelligence. Since the Soviet Union had a secret agent in the person of Kim Philby, who headed all English intelligence directed against her, the U.S.S.R. was aware not only of Hitler's intentions but of Churchill's as well.

On January 30, 1943, the rudest shock of the war came to those in the West, who hoped that the Nazis and Bolsheviks might cancel each other out. At Stalingrad, the Russians finally smashed the Germans, a year and a half before the long-stalled second front of the English and the Americans would officially begin. Stalingrad, the greatest battle in history, marked the beginning of the longest continuous advance in military history—1,500 miles long and upwards of 650 miles wide to Berlin. At Stalingrad, Field Marshal von Paulus, 24 generals, and 330,000 German soldiers were put out of action. Russian losses were very heavy. In just one day, August 23, 1942, 600 German bombers had killed 40,000 of the city's inhabitants.

Now the desire to see Germany overwhelm Russia would not be realized. The second front could no longer be postponed. The North African and Mediterranean campaigns, which were Churchill's means to destroy Bolshevism and preserve the English Empire, had to give way to something more substantial. The Soviet Union could not be hindered from crushing a nationally diseased Germany. Churchill's and Roosevelt's objective was now to save Germany from the Russians—if only a piece of it—and to destroy, as in Dresden, what could not be taken and held by the Western powers.

As the war progressed, the London Poles did not desire a Russian victory over Germany because they feared its effects on the postwar dispositon of Poland. On August 1, 1944, one week after the Soviet Union had announced the formation of a rival government in Lublin that would replace the exile government in London, a segment of the London-inspired army in Warsaw staged a tragic uprising against the Germans that resulted in the deaths of 200,000 Poles. It was an impossible venture from a military standpoint because the uprising could only have succeeded in alliance with the U.S.S.R. Since it was directed militarily against the Germans, and politically against the Russians, it could never have succeeded. This uprising once again demonstrated the lengths to which the narrowly nationalist elite classes would go to further their own ends. As Gabriel Kolko analyzed it: ''The Poles in London claimed to represent Poland on the basis of their prewar party mandates and the dubious 1935 constitution produced after a military coup d'etat. They stood, in brief, for the Old Order and social forces that managed to exist within the framework of an illusion that had not been torn asunder by a war that destroyed six million Poles and physically uprooted and tortured an even larger number.''

Despite the succession of resounding defeats which the Germans had suffered by late 1944, they dreamed of a ''Fourth Reich'' which would replace the now doomed Third Reich. On December 7, 1944, Himmler issued a secret document to the German police and administrative bodies, which stated explicitly that the western territories contained only between 10 and 30 percent pure Germans who could be relied on to build the future ''Fourth Reich.'' Remarkably, the paper was written after Soviet and Polish armies had taken Lublin in July, after the Allies had taken Paris in August, and after the Soviet armies had taken East Prussia in October.

By early 1945, members of the Second Polish Army, together with Soviet forces, were advancing to the Nisa River. On April 16, a battle took place on the right bank of the Nisa in the vicinity of the town of Rotenburg. The retreating enemy units were defending their objectives without regard to losses, for their aim was to impede the passage of General Karol Swierczewski's forces on the other bank. They knew that once the Poles established a bridgehead over the river, Rotenburg would fall and with it a number of other localities.

German soldiers on the Nisa continued shooting only because their propaganda officers had frightened them about what the Russians would do to them if they were captured. Meanwhile, their generals were busily negotiating a separate peace treaty with England and the United States. They sensed that instead of the wealth their leaders had promised them in the form of plunder from the hated Slavs, nothing but defeat loomed ahead for them.

Hard fact could no longer be ignored even by the most unyielding Nazis. Shame was burning in the eyes of those Germans who had to fight on German territory. Their city of Rotenburg had fallen, as they could not hold their lines on the Russian plains or on the Byelorussian, Ukrainian, and Polish fields. Their dream of owning millions of Slavic slaves had evaporated, and the descendants of the Teutonic Knights could already taste the gall of another bitter defeat, as their ancestors had before them at Plowce and Gruenwald.

On the evening of April 16, 1945, the Polish forces captured Rotenburg and continued their push against the weakening but still vicious German fire—this time on the left bank of the Nisa. On this same day, the American forces captured Nuremberg, the cradle of Nazi myth and Hitlerism.

Only ten days later, on April 26, the Soviet and American forces met at the Elbe, greeting each other with a cordial handshake. And on May 1 occurred the last battle of the Soviet and Polish forces for the possession of Berlin, the capital of the Third Reich that its creators had said would last "at least a thousand years."

Early in February, 1945, at Yalta in the Russian Crimea, Churchill, Roosevelt, and Stalin met to discuss further war developments and future policies. Part of a joint declaration issued on February 11 dealt with the question of Polish borders. The Curzon Line was recognized as the eastern frontier of Poland with substantial accessions of territory in the north and west. Insofar as Poland was not represented at Yalta, it was determined that the "opinion" of the new future Polish government "should be sought in due course."

In December, 1942, General Wladyslaw Sikorski of the London exile government had submitted to President Roosevelt a memorandum on the question of the Polish borders along the line of the Oder and Lusatian Nisa. The President agreed to these formulations without reservation. In January, 1943, the Polish ambassador in Britain delivered the same memorandum to the head of the British Foreign Office, who also concurred.

On August 2, 1945, at the Potsdam Conference, Truman, Atlee, and Stalin issued a joint declaration on Germany. This Potsdam Declaration confirmed the agreement of the Allies to establish new Polish-German borders. Yet, a little over a year later, in a speech made on German territory early in September, 1946, Secretary of State James Byrnes reversed the U.S. position in order to support German national interests. Shortly thereafter, on September 16, V. M. Molotov, the Soviet Union's Minister of Foreign Affairs who had been present at all the Big Powers conferences regarding Germany, criticized Byrnes's about-face and concluded that:

> It is obvious what great importance was attached by the Governments of the United States, Great Britain, and the Soviet Union to the decisions concerning the shifting of the western Polish borders, and that in no case did they imply that this decision should be subjected to any revision in the future. . . .
>
>   . . . the three Governments have already given the most practical expression of their attitude towards the western borders by handing Silesia and the above mentioned territories over to the Polish Government and, above all, by accepting the plan of evacuation of the Germans from these territories. Who would have thought that this evacuation of Germans might ever have been considered as a temporary experiment?
>
> The very same persons who undertook to make the decisions providing for the evacuation of Germans from these areas with a view to immediate settlement there of Poles

coming from other parts of Poland cannot now ask for a reversal of their own definite instructions.

The very thought of carrying out such an experiment upon millions of people seems incredible, in view of its cruelty to the Poles as well as to the Germans themselves.

From the above, it is evident that the decision of the Potsdam Conference, signed by Truman, Atlee, and Stalin, has already determined the western Polish borders.

On November 14, 1944, President Roosevelt, in a letter to Stanislaw Mikolajczyk (who assumed leadership of the London Poles upon Sikorski's untimely death that previous July 4), promised to assist Poland materially by resettling the evacuated Germans and by helping to rebuild the western territories. Roosevelt considered it only just that the Germans, who started the war in which they bore clear responsibility for the slaughter of 30 million people, should lose 18 percent of their prewar territory, and that Poland, having lost 46 percent of her land when her eastern border was shifted to the Curzon Line, should be recompensed by the extension of her western border.

Two years after the end of the war, the Moscow Conference of the Big Four foreign ministers once again focussed attention on Germany's postwar borders with France and Poland. By this time, the territory involved had become an integral part of Poland's economy. The Americans and British disagreed with the Russians over the reading of the following paragraph in the Potsdam Declaration: "That, pending the final delimitation of this frontier, the former German territories east of the line running from the Baltic Sea immediately west of Swinoujscie and thence along the Oder River to the confluence of the western Nisa River, and along the western Nisa River to the Czechoslovak frontier, including the portion of East Prussia south of Krolewiec and the territory of the former Free City of Gdansk, shall be placed under the administration of the Polish State."

It is clear that the Potsdam Declaration referred to the territories east of the Oder and Nisa line as "former German territories" and as no longer part of the German state. It also made a clear distinction between these former "German territories" and the rest of Germany which had been placed under the military occupation of the four Allied Powers. Nowhere did the Declaration stipulate, or even suggest, that the Polish administration was only temporary. True, it stated that the final delimitation of the border was still pending. But since Potsdam was not a peace conference, and thus not concerned with the final delimitation of borders, it had to make this reservation. Besides, the term *border delimitation* has a definite meaning in border settlements: to demarcate a border line previously decided upon.

When the Potsdam Agreement was handed over to the Polish delegation at the conference, President Truman gave it a similar interpretation. According to the statement on April 10, 1947, made by the Polish Foreign Minister, the President of the United States declared that "the term 'under Polish administration' was used only for formal reasons because, not being a peace conference, the Three Power Conference in Potsdam had no authority to define the Polish-German border officially." It seemed clear, then, that all parties concerned regarded the Potsdam Agreement as a de facto settlement requiring only formal legalizing by the peace treaty between the victorious Allies and defeated Germany. There never was any doubt as to its finality.

On November 20, 1945, the Four Power Allied Control Council for Germany opened the way for immediate implementation of the Potsdam Declaration by approving a plan for the transfer of the German population from non-German territories into the four zones of occupied Germany.

The evacuation of Germans from Poland—which now included the regained territories in the west—has never, to this day, been protested by any of the victorious powers of World War II. On the basis of Potsdam, Poland assumed its administration and immediately engaged in resettling and rehabilitating the region.

During the war, the Germans had brought hundreds of thousands of Polish slave laborers to the mines, factories, and farms along the Oder and Nisa rivers. Ironically, then, Germans themselves started the process of re-Polanization of these lands.

In the last phase of the war in the east, after Russian and

Polish troops had broken through the German lines in the direction of Berlin, the local German population was evacuated en masse to central Germany. By the time the Russo-Polish forces arrived, the German population was very much reduced, and the Poles were more numerous than before the war. In addition, many Germans voluntarily migrated from these territories even before the Polish authorities began the systematic evacuation of Germans.

Polish slave laborers and remnants of the original Polish population were the first to undertake the arduous task of rehabilitation. Soon, a new stream of Polish settlers began to pour into the newly recovered lands in the west. Most of these were repatriates from east of the Curzon Line, which had been agreed on at Yalta as Poland's eastern border. They were joined by Polish refugees and displaced persons from Germany, Austria, and France; demobilized soldiers from the Polish armies in the west; and many settlers from Poland proper who had been left by the Germans.

No sooner did the war end than the Poles began the enormous task of reconstruction, under the most difficult of conditions. There was no time for despair; everyone set to work. Shipments of food and clothing arrived from the United States and other Western countries not devastated by the war. Commercial exchange transactions and credit extensions were arranged with the Soviet Union. Soviet fish, wool, and flour were bartered for Polish coal. During a two-year period, the American UNRRA delivered articles of necessity worth $481 million. But no one considered handouts as the means to rebuild the country's economy: self-reliant reconstruction would become the means.

The most burning question was that of land reform. The nucleus of the future Polish government, the Polish Committee of National Liberation, in order to compensate the peasants for their losses and to encourage them to devote themselves to more intensive work, decreed that agrarian organization would be based on a strong, sound productive system of small holdings—the private property of their possessors. Thus, at long last was effected the land reform which the Polish peasant had desired for centuries.

Undersized holdings were enlarged to normal standards. New, independent holdings were established by breaking up large private estates, thus giving land to the peasants, workers, agricultural laborers, and small tenants. In all, almost 9,000 estates, with a total area of 4.2 million hectares of land, and 150 agricultural enterprises belonging to 6,724 estate-owning families were affected. Besides the land, the capital to develop it was allocated. In 1947, the peasants received $125 million to restore their farms. This sum was exclusive of relief given them in the form of grain, farm animals, and farm machinery which was extended to 24,000 farm units. In addition, the Peasant Mutual Aid Association organized 1,400 cooperatives and came to own 900 flour mills, 200 distilleries, and a great number of dairies and canning factories. It also organized clubs, libraries, health centers, and farmers' training courses.

The peasants of the western territories received financial aid in the form of long-term credits early in the spring of 1946. Their government also gave them 60,000 tons of seeds, 100,000 tons of potatoes, 10,000 cows, and a few thousand imported horses. Through the Three-Year Plan, in which 20 percent of the national income went into investments, as well as the support of the people, many of whom worked as long as eighteen hours a day, the results in 1946 were highly gratifying. In that year, despite her great losses during the war, Poland reached 56 percent of her prewar agricultural production and 78 percent of her industrial output. The national income reached a par with the prewar year 1938, even though the population had decreased by ten million.

This record was not achieved without some discord—and even sabotage—for a number of German spies and former Gestapo agents with Polish names continued to work for the "Fourth Reich." They were particularly active in the industrial province of Silesia where in September, 1946, in the town of Zabkowice, the factory "Teletechnical Instruments" was put into operation. Plans had been worked out for the production of radios, telephone devices, inductors, condensers, current alternators, and other communication items. The reports that the factory management sent to the Ministry of Industry looked too good: they stated that production not only reached its goal but exceeded it by 25 percent. The Ministry was very pleased indeed and waited impatiently for the products to go on the market in volume. Then suddenly inspectors from the Ministry made an unannounced visit, and when the inspection committee had finished, the matter was turned over to the police. The ensuing investigation revealed that the optimistic reports were false. In reality, the factory had only a few machines in operation; the rest were strewn about in run-down sheds or were rusting in the factory yard. The production quota had not been met; rather, it had failed by a dramatic 90 percent. During a two-month period, only 2,000 unassembled radio and telephone parts had come off the line. But even these few thousand parts were useless, for they had not been made according to specifications.

The losses were found to be caused not by negligence, but by political sabotage by those opposed to Poland's new economy. The head of the factory's directors was an engineer by the name of A. Ferenz, a man of German parentage who had feigned the role of a Polish patriot and had become a member of every local organization in the town. The director of the factory was the engineer, L. Kornilow, a cousin of the notorious White Guard Russian general, who as an officer of the Russian army had escaped to Poland in 1918. The head of the Department of Administration and Distribution was J. Jakubowski, a Reichsdeutsch and a colonel in the German army. Within a month, all three, together with a drove of smaller officials, were brought before a court of justice and were found guilty. The losses, however, had been serious.

As to the final determination of Poland's borders, Poland and the German Democratic Republic reached an agreement on July 6, 1950, which sanctified the Potsdam accord. Twenty years later, the Federal Republic of Germany also recognized the Oder-Nisa border as the legitimate boundary line dividing both Germanies from Poland. Subsequent agreements providing for cooperation along economic and cultural lines have added to the spirit of peace, not only for these countries but for the rest of Europe and the world as well.

Malbork

restored peasant cottage in central Poland

NIEDENTHAL

palace in Wilanow near Warsaw

florian gates in a section of old Cracow

restored buildings in Gdansk

Wroclaw, has been returned to its prewar condition.

The ancient port of Gdansk contains some striking modern housing.

Warsaw, too, has been rebuilt to satisfy a growing need.

MOREK

Warsaw's newest hotel is the skyscraper called the "Forum."

harvesting on a collective farm

MOREK

Each autumn, an international agricultural fair is held in Poznan.

MOREK

This shipyard in Gdynia is called "Paris Commune."

Poland's industrial production continues to expand. J. Filipek was a productivity champion in the zinc and lead mine "Boleslaw" near Olek.

Coal mining is highly sophisticated. This is the operations control room for the mine "JAW" in Slask.

Some industrial operations are precisely individual; this is a crystal worker in Ustron Slaski.

The artist Kamila Piskozub works at restoring a tapestry called "The Hawk and the Pigeon," which hangs in the Wawel Castle in Cracow.

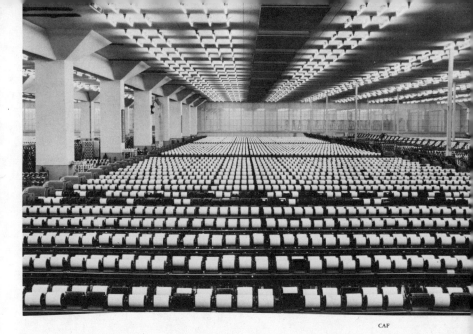

CAF

Complete automation has replaced workers in this spinning factory in Gorzow.

ROSIKOW

The Fiat 126P is produced on assembly lines in Poland.

Poland's Borders Today

BALTIC SEA

POLAND
MAIN ECONOMIC CENTERS

Koszalin
Gdańsk
Elbląg
Szczecin
Olsztyn
Białystok
Gorzów Wkp.
Bydgoszcz
Toruń
Zielona Góra
Poznań
Płock
Wisła
WARSZAWA
Lubin
Łódź
Wrocław
Kielce
Lublin
Odra
Częstochowa
Opole
Tarnobrzeg
Katowice
Mielec
Kraków
Rzeszów
Zakopane

CZECHOSLOVAKIA

USSR

0
50
100
150 km

heavy industry
shipbuilding industry
extraction industry
aviation industry
metallurgy
automotive industry
petro-chemistry
railway rolling stock
cement plant
textile industry

PART II

Chapter 4

sharp silence
springs
upon the ear
and
stings
buzzes within
    my soul
    with
    peasant slyness
    swells
    and sings
preparing for salvation to begin

The true philosopher, I have decided, is the man who under-stands and can live at peace with his family. My American wife Sophia, our two children, and I were on our way to Europe with our sixteen suitcases, most of them filled with gifts for my relatives and childhood friends. It was their first trip abroad and my return after many years to my native Poland.

We were almost ready to leave our apartment in New York for Grand Central Station when my eighteen-year-old son Anthony told me that his younger sister Gloria had pasted some of my poems inside the lid of each suitcase. He opened the first suitcase. I began to read, forgetting everything, caring nothing for other poets. I decided I liked this poem:

from this luxuriant earth
    gold loom of
america
you sprang
seed of carpenter was born again
as once to us two thousand years ago
out of another land
another poverty
christ as humbly born
and from the same enduring
mothers pain . . .

My eleven-year-old daughter was smiling, and in a flash it struck me that her smile expressed a certain satiric wisdom. She said, "I know what you're going to say, but first I want to know what you're thinking."

"Why did you do it?"

"Oh, because of the customs officials."

"Who?"

"For the American, Canadian, English, Polish, French, Italian, and all the other customs officials we'll meet."

"I don't understand."

Brushing aside her straight blond hair, all she answered at first was "Because." With her hair falling over her face she looks sometimes like our friend's Schnauzer. She continued. "We'll be crossing all those borders with our sixteen suitcases, and customs officials will always be looking into them. But when they see the poems inside, they'll read them instead of examining the contents. And the poems are so bad they'll get disgusted and leave us alone. This way we'll save ourselves time and trouble. You told me yourself that we have lots of gifts and so we'll have to pay a lot of duty."

Before I could respond the downstairs bell rang. "That must be Simon," Anthony said.

Whenever we needed someone to take us and our luggage anyplace, we called in Simon.

"I'll never forget," said my son with a grin, "when he was taking us to the country and had too much to drink. He hit the car in front of us and the car in back of us and then he finally hit a tree. The state trooper came and when he asked him for his driver's license, Simon said, 'Officer, be logical, who would give a license for driving like that?' "

"When did this happen?" I was startled.

My wife soothed me—and saved Simon. "We don't have much time. Simon is waiting downstairs."

We brought our valises down to the station wagon as quietly as possible so as not to disturb our neighbors before leaving nor to give our departure away to potential thieves.

In the numb quietness of early dawn we looked at each other

and at our brownstone. Lexington Avenue was deserted as we started on our way to Grand Central Station. The rising sun was only timidly brushing the tops of the brownstones. At the entrance to the subway at Seventy-seventh Street I saw a begger I had spoken to many times before with all his belongings packed into a supermarket cart. I wouldn't have the time to stop and talk with him today, however.

When we got to the station, three redcaps helped us with our valises and we boarded the train bound for Montreal.

As the train came out of the long tunnel hidden under Park Avenue, daylight rushed in through the windows. Soon the sun was shining hotly on suburban dumps full of broken automobiles, refrigerators, mattresses, television sets, and other tokens of our prosperous country.

Later, my wife asked me where our tickets were, and I started searching frantically, convinced that I had lost them. Anthony was no help with his remark, "It will really be something if our railroad and ship tickets are still at home." Just as I began perspiring profusely, to my relief I found the tickets tucked inside our passports. When I found them, I sank down on the seat next to Sophia, who was admiring the scenery.

We were now out of the city and the train gained speed, shaking rhythmically. Our children's eyes were riveted to the landscape. It was their first journey to the land of their forefathers and it was difficult for me to imagine what they could be thinking. My wife had never traveled beyond a few eastern states, so she had lots of questions about life in Poland. But I had no answers as twenty-five years had passed since I had last seen Europe. It was twenty-five years ago too when we were married. We looked at each other now as if we had just met, but our eyes seemed to reflect the closeness of those years. I knew she was excited about this long trip. Against the green background of scenery I saw her faint smile. "I wonder," she said, "how Poland today will compare to the country you left twenty-five years ago?"

I knew what she was thinking. And she knew what I was thinking. "We are going to see my mother," I said, "who enjoys living where she does. We are not going to talk about politics.

What is important about a country is its people. A patriot is someone for whom the best and most important object is man, and who fights for people who are honest with themselves."

"But they can silence you."

"A bell can be silenced, but not a human being. Don't you remember the thousands of people who marched to protest the execution of the Rosenbergs?"

As we reached the Canadian border, there was a knock at our compartment door and two customs officials presented themselves. When they saw the sixteen suitcases they grew pale. The stouter of the two, an American, asked us where we were going.

Our son was the first to reply, "We are going to socialist Poland, first stop."

"And after that, capitalist Europe," said my daughter, staring at the well-pressed uniforms of the two men.

The one, short and fat, gave a brisk order. "Open the suitcases, please."

"All of them?" asked my wife.

"Not all at once. Just one at a time," replied the second official, a tall man with a uniform different from that of the other official. This one was Canadian.

"But there is no room here to open all of them," I interjected. They ignored my polite protest.

"This one, " said the fat official, pointing to the huge Scottish plaid suitcase. Gloria jumped up and began fussing with the belt on the suitcase. I gave her the key and she opened it.

"And what do you have in these suitcases?" I don't remember which one repeated the familiar question.

"Gentlemen, personal things and gifts for our relatives in Poland." What should I have said? Meanwhile, the Canadian official was staring over his friend's shoulder at the inside cover. "Look, what's this?" he asked his partner.

"It's politically subversive, but not illegal. I'll still have to check it out in my book."

The Canadian, seeing my daughter's radiant face, was trying to control his smile. I nearsightedly bent over the suitcase to read Gloria's hieroglyphic endeavors. The American had almost finished reading when the Canadian began to read softly to the steady, pulsating rhythm of the train:

> here
> on earths stormbound crust
> where falsehood swells and rots
> in festering graves
> each chief
> in his own way
> betrays us
> with dictatorial gesture
> mocks our trust
> who has it in his
> heart
> to save us

like whirlpools of black storm water
the rabble surge to the slaughter
where stark humanity stiffens
in infinite lakes of sorrow

> *only a few withstand them*
> *armored by beauty*
> *still loyal*
> *until*
> *the cannon hit squarely*
> *and splintered mankind . . .*

After he finished reading, he said that it reminded him of some good Canadian poetry.

"But read the last part," said the irritated American, "it's propaganda." The Canadian obediently started rereading the poem with an ironic smile that could have been intended for either his colleague or my poem.

"It's a good poem," concluded the Canadian. "Close all the suitcases, and good luck on your voyage."

The American just shook his head, looking mildly exasperated.

At the railroad station in Montreal the bus was waiting to take us to the *Ts/s Stefan Batory* for our transatlantic voyage. The first thing I noticed while traveling through the city toward the pier was that the streets were much cleaner than New York's and that the buildings had more color. The bus driver was friendly and even told us a joke in his French-accented English.

"A young Canadian proposed marriage to a daughter of an American banker. She said that her father wanted to talk with him. The Canadian was good-looking, but poorly dressed. The banker noticed that immediately and asked, how much he was earning.

"The Canadian didn't lose his reason in the face of money. 'Why do you ask? Did I ask you how much you're making?'

"'Oh, this is just a friendly, routine question,' replied the banker, offering him a cigar.

"'You mean your daughter wants to marry me for my money?'"

The whole bus laughed, and then the driver said with sadness in his voice, "And now, ladies and gentlemen, this good-looking Canadian got old and is still driving the same bus in one of the companies of the same banker, so as you probably guessed, he never married the banker's daughter."

This anecdote, I said to myself, would make a good beginning for a fascinating book on Canadian natural resources and manpower and American business.

Chapter 5

a bit of barren land suckled us on
ancestral wormwood
and a brooding mothers tears

now
you
don
an uncivilian suit of green
and substitute the armys regimented
love

today
you wear the epaulets
of scrupulous frauds
adorn yourself with patriotic
shoulder arms
on
to
the
enemy

while i
even in my cradle
no longer believed in
such
a
goal

well i know
that the road to life
lies contrary
that your bullets
are the end of human good
that
in uncensored dawn
must be humanitys
cause

you have
misunderstood
though
you
have a bayonet
and cock feathers in
your hat
and i
  for my law
  of laws
only a kernel of passionate brotherhood

Embarking the *Batory* went smoothly. As we boarded, we heard the sounds of Polish folk tunes floating down from the upper deck. The crew and the captain, we noticed, were very young and as polite to the tourist-class passengers as English and American crews are to first-class passengers. The vessel, weighing just over 14,000 tons, was not large. Inside it was clean and attractively decorated with the paintings and tapestries of leading Polish artists. The furniture was handmade, and the kitchen was as artfully designed as Japanese and Chinese kitchens. The cuisine combined traditional Polish recipes with an exquisite French touch. Because of the many Danish and other Scandinavian travelers on the ship, the menu also featured such basic Danish foods as *bankekød m/kortoffelmos* and *kalvesteg m/gemyse*. For our first dinner we all selected red clear borsch, beluga caviar on toast, filet of wild boar chasseur, and, for dessert, *coupe petit duc*. Gloria drank milk, Anthony green china tea, and my wife and I French coffee with Russian cognac.

Seated at our table were an American businessman of Polish descent who was going to visit his sister in the old country and a doctor returning to Poland after visiting his brother, also a doctor, in New York. The businessman, a man probably over seventy years of age, was short and bald and had embellished his stumpy frame with bracelets, rings, and a gold watch encrusted with diamonds. When he found out that his tablemate was a doctor, he turned to ask, "Doctor, what should I do? I am losing my memory."

"Dear man, you cannot regain that which is lost," replied the doctor. He was a gaunt man with a number tattooed on the same part of the wrist where the merchant had his gold watch clasp. "There's no remedy for it. The best thing you can do is simply to forget about it."

"And this you call the advances of your Polish medicine?"

"And what do the American doctors say about your memory?" asked our son, looking for approval to his mother.

The merchant ignored Anthony's question and changed the subject to wine tasting, revealing, as he sipped and savored, that he was a wholesale butcher who had made good in America. He then returned to his malady and announced that an American wine was the only cure he had found for his memory. I suggested he patent his discovery immediately for, as our best leaders and political thinkers were also afflicted with loss of memory, he could make a fortune.

After dinner the children went to see a Polish film so that they could get acquainted with the language. Meanwhile, my wife and I went up top deck to a clear night on the St. Lawrence River. As the *Batory* glided toward the Atlantic, we saw the Canadian shore houses sparkling like lightning bugs. The clean, refreshing air was exhilarating. As we walked, we passed many couples conversing in English, Danish, French, Polish, and Russian. On this first night on board, everyone seemed happy and animated, and everyone seemed to have something interesting to say. Some of the passengers were returning to Poland for good, some, like us, were going there for a visit, and others were traveling to different parts of Europe. The ship carried almost 1,000 people spread throughout its decks, bars, cabins, exercise rooms, and libraries.

When we returned to our cabin, my thoughts turned to the events of the day, and I pondered writing a poem with a modernistic sea background. But though I admire him, I am not a Conrad. I prefer writing about the solid ground of an almost forgotten Polish countryside, which tonight began to return to memory through the haze of years more clearly than ever before. In the neighboring cabins our daughter and son had gone to sleep after discussing the film they had seen earlier about two young Polish people in a contemporary Polish village and how they coped with the political reforms of the day and the anxieties and strong feelings of adolescence.

On the following morning we awoke to a view of the sun's gold and masses of water and sky which seemed to be in a contest to give off the best blue color. The white liner, traveling now at 20 knots per hour, moved in silent majesty from the St. Lawrence Bay into the Atlantic. At breakfast we were regaled with a dizzying, unending expanse of water and space.

For breakfast our children ordered scrambled eggs Monaco with Polish ham and linden tea. My wife and I chose pike caucasienne, Colombian coffee, fresh strawberries, and hard rolls.

The doctor arrived on time, but our second companion did not appear. Our waiter explained that the businessman had had an accident and would not be able to leave his cabin. The doctor was quiet and somber and did not react to the news. But I was so curious about the businessman's absence that I excused myself and went into the next room to find the waiter, thinking that surely he must know everything about the passengers. I found him carrying a big *corbeille de fruits*. First he told me something about the doctor—that he was a well-known medical scientist originally from Warsaw who won Poland's highest decoration for heroism during the anti-Nazi uprising there. Then, he turned to what had happened to the merchant. It seemed that during the night someone had stolen his diamond-encrusted watch valued at thousands of dollars and that he had reported the theft to the captain. When I returned to table, I remarked to the doctor, "The reason he hasn't come is no reason at all—someone has stolen his watch."

"After breakfast I'll sneak into his cabin," said Gloria, "and I'm sure I'll find the watch in his drawer."

"Don't you dare," warned my wife.

To divert Gloria from her intent, I suggested that we should leave the matter to the ship's officers. And that was the end of it—or so I thought.

After breakfast we went out onto the sundeck. The doctor whispered in my ear, "Normally artists and writers are more sensitive than other people, and I would like to ask you what should be done in a case like this."

"It's simply a matter of a watch disappearing," I responded, "and there's no mystery involved."

"Maybe not," my wife added.

"The sea air is making you as silly as your daughter," I replied.

"I'm afraid I agree with your wife." the doctor said.

"Whatever you think is now academic, for I think our children are already off searching," said Sophia. At that moment, I realized that Gloria and Anthony were no longer on deck.

"Such a theft brings shame to us and the ship's crew," concluded the doctor.

"Time will heal the wound, " I said, slightly annoyed at the doctor's exaggerated sense of morality. My wife, looking at the glass door leading to the bar, added, "But our good doctor wants to use preventive medicine before the wound gets infected."

"That's true," the doctor added. "By complaining and by inactivity we just multiply this malice. I'm going to talk to the captain and explain all the facts to him from the beginning. It's very simple. The man was sitting at our table. We all admired his expensive watch. It disappeared, so to some extent, we are responsible for it."

"There's Gloria," said my wife, looking again through the glass door.

I followed the direction of Sophia's gaze and saw the

businessman sitting at the bar on a high stool drinking some pink liquid. And to my chagrin there was Gloria seated right behind him on a red divan. The bar was full of people, even at this early hour.

"Ask her to come out," I said to my wife.

Sophia went into the bar and tugged at our daughter's red sleeve. But Gloria refused to move. Finally, she took her by the arm and guided her out onto the sundeck. Gloria was in tears. "I almost found the secret of the watch and now I'll never know because of your interference."

"What do you know about it?" we asked.

"I'm not going to tell you, because you've all been so rude to me."

"But it's not nice for you to keep this all a secret. We are all involved in this situation. The ship's personnel is wasting time looking for the watch and here you don't want to tell us." I didn't know whether to believe that Gloria did indeed know anything. It might have been only a child's fantasy.

"I have to figure it out myself, because I don't want to share the reward for finding the watch."

"What kind of reward?" asked Sophia.

"There is no reward," I said, anger mounting in my voice.

But the doctor, a better psychologist than we, said, "Yes, there must be a reward."

From his face I could see that he abhorred tension. My daughter now started on a different tack. "I don't care about the reward. I just want to teach you a lesson, because nobody ever takes me seriously. I'm going to teach you all a lesson."

"You are right," said the doctor.

"Tell us what happened with the watch." I was so angry I could have spanked her.

"Soon after I left you, I saw him walking through the corridors and I followed him. He tripped on the stairs, and you know what?"

"What?"

"His trouser leg ripped and . . . "

"And what?"

"There was a watch on his leg."

"On his leg?"

"Yes, on his leg," Gloria smiled triumphantly.

"But how are we going to see it?" asked the doctor.

There he was, seated at the bar, motionless, holding a glass in both hands. We considered several different approaches. I thought of getting him drunk, while my wife suggested that we should convince him to admit he had made a mistake or else we would tell the captain the truth. But the doctor, believing that the man was determined to embarrass the captain and all the crew, doubted that he would be receptive to either proposal. Finally, we decided that the best solution was to keep after him constantly; we would not let him alone until we saw his watch.

As we started into the bar, he suddenly got up and walked towards us. We met at the entrance and began talking about the beautiful morning and our good sleep. He was pleasant and we were polite. Suddenly our daughter shrieked, "The watch—it's sliding down his leg!"

He bent down phlegmatically and pulled up the left leg of his trousers, saying, "Nothing is sliding down." Now we saw not only one watch on his leg, but four! And we wondered how many he had on the right leg.

At once we realized his game: this enterprising businessman had planned to smuggle the watches into Poland. After our confrontation, he never showed his face again on the voyage; he remained in his cabin and even ate his meals there. And Gloria became a celebrity among us as "the youngest detective."

Later that day, I became better acquainted with the doctor. After so many years, the story of Nazi concentration camps was still written on his face. From the ship's doctor I had learned that his parents, wife, and children perished during the war and that he had been dug out, barely alive, from a tangled pile of corpses at Palmiry Forest where he had miraculously escaped execution. A few weeks after this incident, he was again picked up and was then sent to the Oswiecim concentration camp. There the numbers were burned into his skin. After the war, instead of returning to Warsaw, he settled in the port city of Szczecin where he began practicing medicine again.

When I asked him why he didn't stay with his brother in New York, who had a lucrative medical practice on Fifth Avenue, he replied with simple honesty, "I cannot stand to hold my hand out for a fat office fee when a patient can't or doesn't want to pay; I don't want to be the partner of bill collectors. For me, medicine is the most sacred profession, one whose benefits should be made accessible to the neediest with no regard to financial remuneration."

It was then that I felt I knew just what kind of a man this doctor was. His attitude reminded me of the stubborn character of a Polish farmer whom I used to know before the war. Franciszek Mysliwiec had a plot of land in the village of Sprzecice in Silesia. For twenty years Mysliwiec had won all first prizes in the agricultural fairs of the German chambers of agriculture. His German neighbors kept asking him: "What kind of a Pole are you? You are a citizen of the Third Reich, you live on German soil, you work it like a German, and you have the finest farm in Silesia."

Mysliwiec would then answer his envious neighbors. "Since the time of the first Piasts, Poles have lived in Sprzecice and I too am a Pole. My farm is better than the German ones because Poles work best on their own land; and they can farm more efficiently there than the Germans."

In 1940, the Gestapo tortured him to death at Dachau.

After the war was over, those who survived the occupation set to work on their farms once more despite their hunger. It was very hard at the beginning: they had no shoes, no clothing, not even enough coarse black bread, let alone meat, to eat. There was no fodder for the horses or the other farm animals which had been supplied by the UNRRA or had been brought by their owners from the former Polish region east of the Curzon Line. The old people swelled up and died of hunger; the children were ravaged by tuberculosis.

Later in the voyage, the Atlantic became stormy and the ship was rolling back and forth. I did not feel the effects but Sophia was very seasick. I went down three decks to the ship's hospital to get some pills for her, and in the doorway I met the doctor. "What, is the doctor sick too?"

"Why? Because I come from the hospital? And what will you say when we meet at the gates of the cemetery?" We both laughed. I could see pits and scars in his mouth.

"I don't want to change the subject too quickly," he said, "but I've met someone who has been looking for you."

"Who?"

"Your old friend. A baker from Lodz who considers you a good poet."

"If he does, then he must be my friend. And his name?"

"It's similar to yours. He told me his grandfather and father were also bakers. I was in the concentration camp with him. Now, after a quarter century, we meet here in the corridor of this ship."

"Would you be good enough to take me to him?" I took the doctor by the arm to avoid colliding with the rattling walls. "But first I need some pills for my wife."

A hospital nurse gave me some pills, and the doctor and I took the elevator to the upper deck. I went to my wife, while the doctor left to seek out the baker and bring him to our cabin. To celebrate this special occasion, I rang for the steward and asked him to bring us a bottle of Caucasian champagne and some caviar and crackers. Sophia didn't want the pills, preferring to wait for the champagne. For the next three hours the doctor, the baker and I reminisced about life before the war through champagne and poetry. The baker told us that poetry had helped him through the terrible tragedy of losing a wife and four children in the Second World War. Now, next to his love for his new wife and two sons who had come into his life after the war stood his love for poetry. He could recite the classic Polish pieces as well as the modern poems in Polish, French, Russian, and Yiddish. None of us talked about the war.

At first we exchanged the usual questions one normally asks relatives or friends whom one hasn't seen for a long time. The baker told us that he had just returned from visiting cousins in the Bronx, so I asked why he didn't just settle in the U.S. I was accustomed to personal or political responses to the question, but instead, he began, "I am a religious Jew. I worship as much as I want, and the government gives my rabbi what is needed. No problem there. In America too, no problem in such matters. I like America." And then he hesitated, "but I don't like the long hours in the baker's shop. I have a small business, only four employees. But I can afford a car, a real luxury item in Poland, and a fur coat for my wife. And I am President of the Lodz Bakers Association."

"And your American cousins?" my wife asked.

"My cousins in the Bronx work from five in the morning until ten at night. And what do you think? Do they have a chance to sell a cake to the White House?" He answered his own question, "I get cake orders from the Prime Minister's wife in Warsaw. I have respect in the community."

It was through the baker's good reputation that Sophia and I were invited to sit at the captain's table for the farewell dinner. This honor was bestowed just before we entered the English Channel. The table company consisted of the captain, a Polish journalist and his daughter, an American lawyer of Polish descent, and my wife and me. At dinner we were served cold lobster bellevue, cream of turtle soup with profiterolles, poached salmon daumont, chateaubriand with sauce Bearnaise, *salade Miami*, French compote, *bombe dame blanche*, tart Stephanie, Italian coffee, and *corbeille de fruits*. Everyone on ship had this same meal.

Our dinner conversation centered around children. All of us, except the lawyer who didn't have any, raved about our respective children. During the remaining days on board, however, I didn't see very much of my children, as they were busy seeing their new friends for the last time. Gloria had been teaching English to a girl who in exchange was giving Gloria Polish lessons. One day the girl's mother told us that her daughter had quarreled with Gloria. My wife remarked, "How can they quarrel if they don't know each other's language?"

The woman replied, "Because they're children, and they don't need language to quarrel."

And I added, "They're obviously training to be grownups."

Anthony, aside from swimming, pingpong, and other

sports, was also becoming acquainted with American, French, and Polish girls.

On the very first day of our sail, I had discovered that postwar youth are no different from youth of my generation. As always, their main concerns are to have a good time and adventures in love and to share their romantic notions about their daily lives. Today, however, there is more communion among youth worldwide than in my day; they are better organized internationally than the Roman Catholic Church. They protest the misery around them. They no longer fear hell, nor do they believe in an ecclesiastical heaven. Their music has brought them together.

We could observe today's youth, full of suprises and nervous tricks, as we moved slowly over the dark turbulent waters of the North Sea. At Southampton we said goodbye to many of the French and English passengers and now found ourselves mostly among Danish, Polish, and Soviet citizens. We exchanged addresses and even received an invitation from a pleasant Danish farmer to visit him at his homestead near Copenhagen. He was so persistent that we told him we would visit him on our way back if we had the time and did not go to the Soviet Union.

When the *Batory* docked at Copenhagen, it was a sunny day but our Danish friend had tears in his eyes and we were sad. Again, he asked for assurance that we would visit him on his farm. I liked this easy-going, honest man. Like so many of us, he had suffered the ravages of war. He had lost his brother and, as a result, had become a pacifist. Thus it was that I recited to him the poem about two brothers that is reproduced at the beginning of this chapter.

Chapter 6

by some mischance
of pride
   or petulance
in fossil forests of remembrance
we must stand
where
   shorn boughs
   like gnarled hands
   point our severed paths
whose
straggling tracks
go separate
and
blind

        thus in our hearts blood
        under our young heels
        our fate lies prone

while life marshals us all
you
and
the
trees
and
i
into the night alone
yet
there is something stays
      intangible and real
while we like fickle winds deceive the grove
still
  the leaves hold your ageless glint of eyes
 still
   earth is drenched with ancient scent of love

When the *Batory* entered the Baltic Sea, we still could not see land, but, what joy, I knew I was breathing Polish air again. The ship was filled with the sounds of our fellow voyagers discussing our imminent arrival. The captain proudly pointed out a Polish school ship passing in the distance. We could even make out its name—*Dar Pomorza*. According to the captain, she was transporting nearly 100 navigation students on a trip of 10,000 sea-miles. He also told us of a group of ten geographers and navigators who had recently left the port of Szczecin on the *Smialy* for a long trip around the tip of South America to make geomorphological, oceanological, and climatological studies. Poland's shipping has made a great recovery after the loss of all her ships and many sea specialists and sailors during the Second World War.

In comparing contemporary Poland's economic and social conditions with those of other countries, what must be kept constantly in mind is her catastrophic economic situation immediately after liberation by the Soviet and Polish armies. Her present economic and social problems are more the consequence of the war (which left six million dead and necessitated the rebuilding of practically everything from scratch) than any other single factor. During the war, Poland lost the equivalent in material value of one half of the U.S. gross national product in 1929, at which time Poland had only one-quarter the U.S. population. Much of her industry was destroyed, and whatever remained was deprived of raw and auxiliary materials and fuel. Postwar, all forms of economic organization were in a state of collapse, and there were great numbers of ownerless, abandoned factories. Everything was at a standstill; hence, there was almost complete unemployment among the Polish working class.

Rural areas were without livestock and a great part of their food supply. They were also devastated by military operations. Provision stores in the larger towns were empty, and there was danger of famine, except in the western territories where, because of their swift retreat, the Germans had been unable to wreak further destruction. Commerce, including transport and communications, was either nonexistent or disorganized.

In addition to this trade paralysis, there was an enormous quantity of paper money, which the Germans deliberately increased in amount during the last month of their occupation so as to promote financial chaos. Poland's situation was made yet more desperate when the country was divided into two different economic units consisting of the former "General Government" and the territories incorporated into the Reich, each of which had different pricing and measuring levels.

In summary, at the moment of liberation, there was almost complete unemployment, real danger of famine, general lack of transportation, and chaos in ownership, organization, and finance. But during the succeeding twenty years, the entire economy was rebuilt so that Polish ports like Gdansk, Gdynia, and Szczecin were once more the equal of ports in the rest of the developed world. (By 1975, the amount of cargo loaded had reached thirty million tons.)

But all thoughts of statistics ceased when I saw land and the ship slowly turned to enter the port. My children were very excited. They began counting how many ships had foreign flags; they had reached forty-four when we got a view of the city of Gdynia in detail.

As we disembarked, we noted that the city appeared to have been built in a day, for we could smell fresh cement and see countless workers on scaffolding constructing brick buildings. Docks and streets swarmed with people. My family looked out among them for faces resembling mine since we knew my brothers would be there. I stood with Sophia, Gloria, and Anthony, overwhelmed and speechless. So many years had elapsed and so much bitterness had accumulated since I last saw Poland. Leaving one's native country is like leaving a woman—a short separation stimulates love, but a long absence breeds only despair.

It is difficult for me now to express the feelings that welled up in me at that moment for the people, the land, and the sun and sea which I had left so long ago. Poetry is the only medium which can accurately convey the emotions that flooded my soul at this my first sight of my beloved Poland in twenty-five years:

today it is no fear
and no despair
    that prompts our
    feeble scribble

neither as in the past
    our common past
out there
do we begin with
invocation
of
the gods

today we will not
beat our heads against the wall
and curse

nor dream of you
at night
and sob
    though we have
    heart for it
    and almost
    certain right

what were
    the use
what were
    the use

we will no more
recite agelong
our litany of wrong
torture the national
conscience
till
it
writhe

and for our
old loves sake
we ask apology
no longer

how many springs
have passed
in petaled
stars
what silver winters
stark
as the paupers
hunger

we forgive you
merciless one
who drove us forth with scarred
and swollen hands

our only shirt
the strangers tithe
yet you had bread
and happiness
to feed
us
all

had
you
but felt
the peasants honest fervor
looked once into his soul
misled you
figured up
your purses
fill

we
left
you
never
knew
and only
death
can
now
return
us
to
you
yet this you owe us
by the earnest will
that offered you our
generous hands and hearts
you took the first
for toil and spurned
the latter
it is no matter
but by the right
of bloodsweat agony
> *we ask imperiously*
> *that bread make sweet your land*
> *your fields bear*
> *bloom unmarred*
> *and*
> *that our brothers*
> *breathe*
> *free*
> *heaven undeterred*
these words our bitterness
dictates who are
in an alien place
scarred by your every
scar

and
who on saint days
to wish you good
our filial prayer
your strength
and
the
wise might
of
brotherhood

My reflections on my homeland were interrupted by Gloria's joyful exclamation: "Look at the old man with the white beard and mustache! The one between the bouquets of flowers!"

"Yes. So?" repeated my wife and son.

"Doesn't he look like your father?"

"But he's no longer alive." I was strongly shaken now.

"You're wrong," Gloria persisted. "He must be alive, he's waving his hands to you." Before I could get a good look at him, the old man had disappeared into the teeming throng and we never saw him again.

We proceeded to a vast customs building. Contrary to some officials I had met elsewhere, these customs men were very polite. When confronted with our suitcases, one fellow asked Anthony to open the green one. He looked at the poem pasted inside the cover without questioning and at the blue, red, and green dresses of my wife and daughter. He then inquired into the contents of the other fifteen suitcases, and Gloria quickly answered: "The same stuff." To our surprise he seemed satisfied and told us we didn't have to open them.

We called for porters who took the suitcases outside and put them into two taxis. As we left the customs building, my youngest brother, Gienek, a captain in the Polish army, was waiting with two bouquets of roses for Sophia and Gloria. They recognized him as soon as they saw him. They thought he looked like me when I was younger. After a tear-filled greeting, we learned that he had traveled all night from the western section of the country and had been waiting at the port for many hours. Because of this all-night ride, he had decided not to bring the rest of his family, my mother, and my other brothers.

As we were all hungry, we began walking to a nearby restaurant. But he stopped us, explaining that the best restaurants were located in Gdansk. We took a taxi to the Monopol Hotel in Gdansk, where, in a modern dining room with a fine view of the city, we dined on mushroom soup, pork chops, two kinds of salad, fresh strawberries, and mineral water.

When I tried to pay the bill, the waitress would not accept my dollars; she insisted on *zlotys*. My brother started counting his money, but discovered he didn't have enough to cover the bill. Just then a tall, baldish man with a plump, brunette woman stood up from the table next to ours and graciously announced that he would lend us a few thousand *zlotys* until we were able to exchange our currency.

We were so moved by their kindness that we invited them to join us at our table, where we introduced ourselves. He told us that he was a professor of psychology at Warsaw University and that his wife was a doctor of medicine. I took out my pipe and tried to light it with Polish matches. To everyone's amusement I was not successful. The professor then related a story about his friend, also a pipe smoker, who once had a summer home. An accident with his small gasoline stove caused a fire which completely destroyed his house. The next day, as he was cleaning up the debris, he discovered that everything had burned except a box of Polish matches.

My brother was brimming with information and began telling my children the history of the Baltic seacoast. The conversation was so interesting that we decided to prolong it in a walk through Gdansk. The streets looked like medieval scenes in a colorful storybook. Dlugi Targ Street was especially beautiful with its many historic buildings restored in every detail to their original state. We marveled at the gilded stairways and gold tracings on the pink- and blue-fronted buildings. When Anthony asked for more information on the port's facilities, his uncle noted that Gdansk and Poland's other two leading ports were served by almost 200 cranes, including grasping bridge-cranes and powerful floating river-cranes with 100-ton lifting power. Conveyor belts loaded coal onto vast transport ships that were guided out of the harbor by tugboats. He added, "As you can see, they are in the process of building new automated docking and making more room for storage space."

Gloria, who plays the guitar and piano, was very much interested in the International Festival of Songs which is conducted every year in Sopot, the Baltic summer resort. She asked her uncle whether it was true that Americans would take part in the festival that year.

"I don't know," he responded, "but I read in the papers that Canada will be participating again this year. Last year, a Canadian song won second place."

My brother was obviously proud of his country, and his nephew and niece were providing him with the ideal opportunity for pointing out Poland's virtues.

"Sopot has been famous for a thousand years for something else," he said.

"For the sand," replied Anthony.

"Yes and no. It is not the sand which you see now," he began. "A thousand years ago Sopot was encircled with a stucco wall, and inside of this wall the inhabitants made jewelry and decorations from amber. More and more people all over the world came to buy amber every year, and not just merchants, but ordinary people too."

In the evening, as the cold wind swept in off the sea and the sun projected its final golden rays onto the turbulent waters, we left the picturesque Baltic shore and traveled by train into the Lublin District where my mother lived in the little village of Sitno. The passengers and the train's crew were pleasant, and I observed that they appeared much more willing to help and greet one another than in New York City. Encouraged by their friendliness, we invited the conductor of our car for a glass of Okocim beer and sausages. He was a short, skinny man of about forty-five with brown hair and fast-moving brown eyes. He was dressed in a dark blue uniform, similar to that worn by American conductors. We discovered that he had spent his youth in the eastern part of Poland and was now living in the capital with his wife and four children. He mentioned that he made only 3,500 *zlotys* a month and that all of his children were in school, ranging from high school to the university. Amazed, Sophia asked him how he could afford it, for one dollar equaled thirty-three *zlotys*.

"Very simple," he explained. "My children are good students and all of them are on state scholarships; my apartment, car, and electricity cost me only as much as your pennies. The children receive all-expense-paid vacations. My wife also works, and her salary goes into the bank because we eventually want to buy a summer home."

"So," I said, "You have arranged your life well."

"I can't complain. I have long hours and can't be home too often, but my situation is so much better than that of my father who was a railroad worker before the war. He didn't have free medicine or hospitalization or a four-week paid vacation. I get my uniforms free, too."

In his wanderings through the train, Anthony met an eighteen-year-old girl from the American Midwest who had been touring Europe for a year and a half and who was interested in commercial drawing. She told him of her amazement at the disparity between what she had read about Poland in the States and what she had seen in her travels. As an artist, she felt this could be expressed in the difference between the color gray and the rainbow.

It was early in the morning when we got off the train at Zamosc. We were immediately engulfed by a crowd of young people carrying a variety of suitcases, traveling bags, and knapsacks. They were coming from many directions for an outing, and all of them wore green scout uniforms. We soon learned that camping is the national pastime of the young. We made our way through this cheerful crowd with all our baggage to the station exit. There we hoped to find three taxis to take us the ten miles to the house where my mother lived with my farmer brother and his wife and three children.

A policeman, spotting us for tourists, approached, telling us,

"You will wait all day for taxis. You should know this is a small town."

"What should I do then?" I asked.

"In a few minutes another policeman takes over my shift and I will go to the center of town myself and find three taxis for you."

I wondered how much this favor would cost us but discreetly I said nothing.

After about a ten-minute wait, we saw three taxis coming toward us. In the first one, next to the driver, sat our policeman. He got out and said, "Here are your taxis. Have a nice time in our village." He touched his cap and left quickly.

I took a dollar bill and two packs of cigarettes from my wife's handbag and ran after him. He looked at my outstretched hand and said, "Maybe in your country the police expect to be paid for such favors, but not in mine." He didn't look at me again, but just turned and left.

Sophia and I rode in the first taxi with our four suitcases, enjoying the country scene. Our driver, a young man, was poorly dressed but clean and smooth-shaven. As we drove slowly along, he pointed out the site of a fierce battle between the Polish and German armies during the last war. Through the thick foliage and slender young trees we could see the ruins of buildings and a large cemetery where fresh flowers had been placed on the graves by the villagers. I was reminded of a poem by Leon Pasternak, whom I expected to see in Warsaw sometime later.

The time will come—a return of the time of plowing but to plow
The left lava of war. A forest will rise from the bone of the
       ground.
Fern will soothe the blue stumps. Only decayed wood
With vampire eyes will pierce the night and suck
       remembrance up.
O the escaped years, how they dash themselves to oblivion
Where flames of an earth-created hell funneled to high
       heaven,
Cool lakes now lie, unfurl the gold of swimming lilies.

Peace, peace over the earth! Deep the plow drives
And gathers up the remnant hatred of a sordid time,
Strange remains—here disclosed the fossil hand, joints
Still wedded to its trigger, with never release from locked
Violent stubbornness. Here are men, bleak limbs
In clinch of battle, though but discard of disheveled bones.
A thorax endures its killing blade, with terrible crop of
     teeth
Chokes an adversary's time-congealed and foreign cry.
Invader dead, and close by—the conquered iron cross.
The cross which dedicates its hollow of gained ground with
     rust.

Where hesitant you now relinquish secret of your longings,
Pause awhile, and remember the hatred of our inhumanity.
Thanks to her you find a smile, and hear the call of a bird,
And you stand at night by the open window, held by the
     gentle voice
Of a violin. And full of peace you walk, all unknowing
Tread the dark plots of a war, for here are honeyed fields.
You sing your passage through the forest, hair stroking the
     leaves.
The handsome world about you seems a free gift and wide.

The sun was already high when we stopped in front of Mother's shingled white house shaded on three sides by a flower-strewn orchard. I walked down the narrow path, followed by my wife, children, and brother. I wanted to go in through the back door. The large courtyard was bordered on three sides by barns for the domestic animals. In the yard were a brown and white spotted cow and many chickens of all colors and sizes. I walked into the kitchen and saw an old woman of about five feet seven wearing a dark green dress. She raised her blue eyes from her cooking utensils, and the spoon dropped from her hand. She threw her arms around my neck without a word . . . It might have been a minute or more—we weren't aware of the time. My wife, standing to the side, gently said, "Let us greet your mother too."

Then my brother Wladek, the only farmer in the family, came in with his wife and their three children, aged seven to sixteen. We all embraced. Suddenly we smelled burning vegetables.

"Oh, my soup is burning!" My mother looked into her big black kettle and announced that the soup was indeed burned. "But so, what is soup?" she said. "We have guests whom I never expected to live to see." With those words she sat down at the kitchen table and began to sob.

We left her alone for a few minutes and went back to the cars to help the taxi drivers carry the suitcases into the house. When they left, my mother remarked that we must be very hungry and without waiting for a reply ordered us into the big room to sit down while she prepared something to eat.

Wladek opened the door and fresh air rushed into a large room about twenty-five feet long and twenty-five feet wide. Its six big windows were decorated with handmade red and white curtains. My sister-in-law, who was walking in front of me, stepped aside and said she would help Mother prepare the meal. Sophia went with her.

Before we could begin any kind of conversation, Wladek asked his oldest child, his only son, to bring some vodka, kielbasa, and bread from the kitchen. At this moment his wife popped her head in to say, "Hey, hero, come to the kitchen and chop off the chicken's head. We don't have the courage. And hurry, we have to eat."

"Why do you call him 'hero'?" I asked.

His son interrupted, "Because he got medals for fighting Nazis. When our mother is in a good mood, she calls Papa a hero."

My brother followed his wife, but paused long enough in the doorway to explain, "I don't know what's the matter with me. During the war I did all kinds of things a man defending his country is supposed to do. But today I can't stand the sight of blood—I hate killing the chickens."

While we waited for the meal, we talked about friends and relatives who had perished during the war. This sad talk was interrupted by a surprise for me. Jan Furtak, whom my brother had invited for lunch, arrived. He had been a friend of the family since before the war. He was the only nonrelative invited. Before the war as a young man he supported himself with odd jobs. One day, passing the gardens of the local count, Jan stole some cherries. The count fired on him and blinded him for life.

Of course, the count was not brought to justice, for the law was on his side. Before the war, in this land as in America, private property was a sacred possession which was given more protection under the law than people were. In addition to being blinded, Jan was also thrown into jail. It was only a few years ago that the village council sent him to Warsaw to learn Braille. He is now a teacher in a school for the blind. Thousands of other handicapped people like Jan, as well as those who were crippled by the Germans, have had to be reeducated and have now been placed in constructive jobs throughout the country.

Before we had a chance for much talk the meal was ready. For lunch we had stuffed chicken, small parslied potatoes, mushrooms fried in butter and sour cream, a garden salad, and, for dessert, wild strawberries and Cuban coffee. My mother, who does not drink, looked disapprovingly as the vodka was brought in. She ate little. Instead, she was quietly observing my family and asking all sorts of questions about the difference in life styles in America.

"Do you have sparrows in New York? Are they the same as here?"

"Yes, we have sparrows. But I have to admit they are smaller and thinner, though they're the same color."

At this moment my seven-year-old niece interjected, "Probably the long trip to New York made them thin and unhappy."

A heavy rain started beating on the windows. It might have been raining for a while, but only then did I notice it.

"I would like to drive you to our father's grave," Wladek said, "but we had better wait until this terrible rain stops."

"It will stop," Mother said. "This rain is for the flowers I planted last week on his grave." She looked at the window to confirm her prediction. "It will stop very soon; then we will go."

Outside it was very gray and dark. I went to the door to peer out, saying to myself, "I have to look at Polish weather which I've completely forgotten about."

When the rain let up, my mother and I went together into the courtyard. While the rain had lessened, the wind was growing stronger. The trees were swaying violently, a grayish mist covering everything around us. I looked at the heavy, leaden skies looming above and shivered. Mother took me by the hand, whispering, "Probably the Almighty is angry, because instead of going to the grave of your father we sat and had lunch." I said nothing and turned my gaze again to the sky.

On our way back from the courtyard Mother reminded me of how fond father had been of my writing and how seriously he used to take it.

"I know that," I said. "I only wish I had had a chance to see him before he died."

Tears appeared in her eyes. "He was waiting to see you but he died in Warsaw. We brought him here because he wanted to be buried in the village." She wiped her face with her apron.

We stood together quietly, she lost in her own private thoughts and I recalling the first poem I had dedicated to my father:

> *against the tyrannical*
> *like blood gushing scarlet from*
> *the pierced heart*
> *spurts red my protest*
> *my soul is churchless but my*
> *heart like a bell rings pure*
> *homo perpetuus i write with sure*
> *stroke our ache for luckier*
> *generations*
> *to attest*

The rain stopped. My mother said, "You see, in one more minute we'll have the sun."

"Yes, we will. You know the skies better than anyone else in this village."

"Don't flatter me, now," she said warmly. "Let's go inside. They are waiting for us." And she began to lead the way.

When we reappeared in the kitchen, my youngest niece Grazyna was washing her face.

"Why are you washing only one ear?" asked er grandmother. The little girl looked up from the large washbowl and explained. "I wash my left ear all the time because the teacher passes between the benches and only inspects one ear."

"Don't you think I have a bright granddaughter?" A smile appeared on my mother's tired face. "She's very smart at school. She's even learning music."

"What instrument and where is she studying?" I asked.

"The *mazanki*. She plays every afternoon in school. We have a very famous folk musician named Tomasz Sliwa here in town. He teaches in a state music school. He plays the *manzanki*, the bagpipes, and *siesienki*. He even makes the instruments himself. Other schools and places buy them. Students come from all over the country to learn his folk music."

"Tell me though," I asked my niece, "Why are you learning to play on only a three-stringed violin?"

"It will be easy for me to go from three strings to the piano."

"You see," said Mother, "she always has an answer. A few days ago her mother scolded her for having a dirty face at the dinner table. And she replied, 'If I had as many faces as I have dresses, then could I keep them from getting dirty?'"

I wondered how far this little peasant girl would go in a country where education is free, where state scholarships cover not only housing for over half of all students but also food, clothing, and books, and where the rate of attendance is proportionally higher than in England or either of the two Germanies.

Not far from my family's village is Lublin Catholic University, which I was to visit in our stay. It was destroyed during the Nazi occupation and was entirely rebuilt after the war. With governmental assistance, it became the first university to resume normal classes. During the last twenty years, this university has produced many impressive scientific achievements. In 1975, 2,600 students were enrolled, a quarter of whom were in the theological school. There were 60 full professors and 150 assistant professors. Students take an active part in various scientific groups, interschoolastic seminars, and national symposia. Graduates are employed in educational centers, scientific institutes, and state administrative agencies. However, the greatest need for graduates is in church institutions and Catholic movement associations. In the last twenty years 1,500 clergy have been graduated, 380 of whom have taken doctoral degrees; at present there are 600 priests and nuns enrolled.

Along with the Catholic Theological Academy in Warsaw, the university has become a main center of ecclesiastical scholarship. It also has a major role in the country's scientific life and maintains contacts with international scientific organizations. As an example of the university's creative vitality, in one year the faculty wrote 400 papers and books. The university library contains 500,000 volumes, while the twenty-nine departments have their own libraries totaling 150,000 volumes. This Catholic university also shares in research directed by the Polish Academy of Sciences.

In addition to the university, Lublin has many historical buildings and landmarks, which have been restored and are now carefully preserved. Beneath the old section of the city is a network of passages and corridors which in some places is several stories deep. From time to time, one hears tales about these passages; a horse and cart disappear from the street, or men working in a cellar fall two stories into the caverns. About ten years ago, the city fathers and a Warsaw organization called the *Geoprojekt* explored and mapped these ancient caverns and published a commentary about them. Their history begins in the first quarter of the fourteenth century, when King Wladyslaw Lokietek granted city rights to the village of Lublin because of its geographical and commercial position as a link between east and west. Commerce and industry flourished, and because of its prosperity Lublin suffered attacks from the Tartars and other nomadic tribes. As a defense against these plunderers, a system of canals and passageways was built under the city. Almost every house under the old part of the city had vast cellars in which today one could park a number of large trucks. Not long ago engineers examined these cellars and found barrels of wine and honey, tattered silk, brocade, and even some jewelry, all well hidden behind walls ten feet high. Under Podwale, Krolewska, and Zielona streets, archeologists from Warsaw University uncovered well-preserved caskets containing human skeletons wrapped in colorful cloth and elaborate jewelry. Some of the passageways served as temporary housing and contained basic domestic implements, including some very fine pottery. Excavation and examination of these networks are incomplete, and many historical secrets are still undiscovered. During our visit we saw a sinking tree on Litewski Place and on Wincenty Pol Street a house that had cracked as one side had sunk into the ground.

Before we left for the cemetery and my father's grave, a group of children with bouquets of flowers came up to us. As I found out from my mother, my nephew and nieces had asked them to come as a welcome to their guests from America. I gave some presents to the children, who were dressed in brightly colored costumes and their Sunday shoes. This scene called to mind a poem written by Jan Galkowski, one of the younger group of writers who began publishing in national magazines just after the Second World War:

> *Your little head I stroked—*
> *Felt your hair*
> *More melting soft than chickling's down.*
> *Your eyes*
> *So crowded with joys*
> *I no longer believe in wars.*
> *I will take your little shoes to the shoeman—*
> *Soon you will go to school a growing boy.*

I know how you cuddle the cat
Many's the time
He pats you with his puffed paws
So puzzled he is
By the small person
Who is happy when walking on all fours.
I know your delight in the sparrow
So drab he is
And so much fatter than a fly.
And only some day will you learn
That there are those
Who seeing even a child in need will pass
    him by.
You love all people
Knowing only the goodness that their faces
    keep,
And how bright your laughter
When they try to scare you
Dressed as a gypsy or a chimney-sweep.

From out of the golden river's hand
Each crumb of brightness spills
For you to build a home.
A hill goes up
Out of golden sand
With doors of mussel shells
And shining windows of pebbles.
Already there's a roof
And chimneys of small sea rubble
And you lift your eyes:
Over the house
Is a real heaven
Of river-wind, blown wonderful.
Sudden wings overhead
But not to hurt your little house
—just a laughing gull.

The sun was receding behind the orchard when Wladek brought out his wagon drawn by two handsome black horses. We got in and set out on the main village road for the cemetery. On both sides of the road we noticed that nearly every second house was new, built with bricks and roofed with shingles. On some of the roofs we noticed television antennas. Around every house were orchards and flower gardens, and behind them extended strips of ripe rye, barley, or wheat. On the road a small herd of cattle passed, with motorcycles and cars snaking through them. Men and women were coming from the fields. They were dressed in gray working clothes, and for a touch of color the women had added flowered kerchiefs.

"And where is your collectivization?" I asked Wladek.

"We don't have it in our village. But there are state farms and cooperative farms in various parts of the country, and I can assure you they are producing more than we 'prywatni.'"

"So why don't you join them?"

"I was raised like this and have no strength to start up a cooperative farm in our village. But if we could combine all the farms in our village into one big cooperative, get machines from the state, and work scientifically, I am sure each farmer would get better profits because we would be producing more."

"How many cooperative farms are there in Poland?"

"It is difficult to estimate because some of the cooperatives have been dissolved and a new cooperative is frequently organized in a neighboring village. But I think there are about 1,500. In addition, we have state-operated farms. I think these make up 15 percent of the total national farmland."

"That's not that much," I commented.

"Yes, you're right, not much, but everything is voluntary; no one is compelled to participate. As you know, the small farm in our country today is inefficient since it is still largely dependent on horse and human power. We have to work very hard to make a living, whereas on a state farm or a cooperative your work and recreation is equally divided among all the people. The farming is mechanized and based on modern scientific principles. Farm experts are constantly helping to produce better grades of livestock, so that by the end of the year there is more to sell, and of course, more profit for all the members collectively."

"How do you think you children will decide?"

"I don't know about my daughters—they are still too young, but next year my son is going to agricultural college to study animal husbandry. As he loves horses so much, he will go to some state farm where they breed horses for foreign export. And besides that, a majority of Polish youth today is socially minded and tries to participate in the state's economic enterprises."

The red sun had passed behind the edge of the horizon when we reached the huge maple trees bordering the cemetery. My brother was the first to jump off the wagon, taking out two bags of oats for the horses. I looked at the scenery, green and peaceful and stirring with life. Evening was upon us.

As we started to walk to my father's grave, I remembered how he would hide books that he had taken from the nobleman's estate for whom he did occasional work. It was my father's love for books that no doubt stimulated my passion for the printed word. Every spare moment that I was not doing farm work, I used to nestle myself in a cool heap of hay in the barn, lost in fantasy and imagination with my books.

I followed my mother in silence to the center of the cemetery where my father was buried. Ancient maple, acacia, and pine trees guarded the resting place of a few thousand people. When we reached the grave, my mother started digging in the surrounding flowers to hide her tears. I also had tears in my eyes.

Chapter 7

He did not choose to take you, and yet the play
Of your inspired perceptions, alive with rays
Of light like guarding angel hands, come round
And hedge you with great choirs of heaven sound.
You loved the world and free was the air you
  breathed
But terror has come, and you go not unscathed
And still more terrible torture of the lord
You knew as your great creative soul scarred.
Your modest bronze so hid your fame
That to touch it was to feel the flame
Rekindled of your rose-bright psalm.
Till up struck a raging arrogant arm,
Clawed at your stately calm, bestial, obscene
Smashed your presence to kill what you had been.
Heavy your deathbed words on the murderer's head:
"Pierce me through the heart when I lie dead.
For me no last clutch beneath the ground
Of breath," you said. Now you are one wound.
They have in the blindness carried out their part,
For the whole world you loved lay in your heart,
And that world now thrust through. Though you saved!
Not dark thrust into any writhing grave,
But alive for storms—god of the clashing air!
Great Funeral March—the play of a world's despair.

This poem, "The Destruction of Chopin's Monument by the Nazis," was written by Leopold Staff, the greatest Polish poet between the two world wars. He was a conservative man who believed in art for art's sake. The Nazi atrocities left their mark on his work and brought him closer to the current problems of a socialist country.

112

By the time we left the cemetery, night was descending upon the village. The road was empty and from the gardens the sweet scent of flowers filled the air. Electric lights illuminated the windows of all the houses. I remembered that before the war this same village used only kerosene lamps. When we reached the center of the village, we could hear loud music played by the local orchestra. Although it was only June 26, Wladek informed me that the people of the town were already preparing for July 22—the National Celebration of Freedom from the Nazis. He explained that on the appointed day Mass would be celebrated in the local church and afterwards a procession would go from the church to the brick school building where a teacher and a priest would give speeches. Later, the school children would perform dances and the village dramatic circle would present their play. After the official ceremony, all the young traditionally eat, dance, and sing until sunrise.

We were tired and, when we arrived home, we prepared immediately for bed. Wladek and his wife gave us their bedroom. They, their family, and my children slept in the barn in the hay. It had been a very long day but before we fell asleep Sophia and I wrote a poem in which we tried to evoke the feeling of an evening in a rustic hut:

> *out of the steamy stupor of the room*
> *drunk with the fume of flesh*
> *the dream grew*
> *on the warm humped rafters*
> *blazed from the saint unseen in shadowed frame*
> *glittered on redlit window panes*
> *the walls*
> *spun round*
> *turned upside down*
> *the heart*
> *snuggled in*
> *soft bliss*
> *while down the flue*
> *stars rained*
> *till all the hearth was silverstained*

the snoring louts that night
were openmouthed
in wonder at the sight

When we got up in the morning, we were surprised to see the table in our room covered with a white linen cloth. On top of it, looking very appetizing, were freshly baked black bread, perhaps a dozen eggs, a slab of ham, a round piece of butter, and slices of farmer's cheese with caraway seeds. In the middle of the table stood a huge bowl of cherries, and around the edges of the table were glasses full of milk and cups of coffee. We began eating immediately. It seemed that we had never tasted more delicious bread. It was so good because, unlike bread in America, all the ingredients were natural.

We looked out the window and saw more than a hundred chickens fluttering around my attractive sister-in-law, who was tossing grain and bread crumbs from her red apron. Meanwhile, my brother Wladek was watering the horses from the well at the edge of the courtyard. This sight brought back my youth so vividly that I found myself going outside and cutting some fresh grass for them with the scythe. This used to be my household chore thirty years ago. But this time it was different: my family stood around me, very curious to see whether I could still handle the tool. The sun shot brilliant gold rays over the green pasture, and as I passed the barn I heard the sparrows chirping and the lark singing his melody. My mother, who was behind me, remarked happily, "I have a feeling that we will have good weather this summer and a good harvest." My arms felt good and young again as the tall grass crackled and swished under my long strokes.

That day, under the pressure of all the excitement, our mother was taken ill. Her varicose veins on both legs opened, and we had trouble stopping the hemorrhaging. We called for the village doctor, a most efficient woman, who examined her and told her to remain in bed. But Mother wanted to be taken to the hospital. As we were going to visit Warsaw next, Mother asked to be taken to the hospital there.

Toward evening, with the doctor's approval, we left for the railroad station in Zamosc. We went by horsedrawn cart. As we approached Zamosc, we saw its sixteenth-century town hall which seemed to illuminate much of the town. Zamosc played a very important role in the cultural and economic life of early Poland. Today it and the entire Lublin district are filled with historical monuments, many of which date from the sixteenth century, when the powerful magnate and Polish political leader Jan Zamoyski brought in the Italian architect Bernardino Morendi to plan a city as a centerpiece for his many possessions. Today nothing is left of Hetman Jan Zamoyski's power and nobody remembers much about him. But the beautiful town is still standing. In and around the ruins of its medieval walls new houses were being constructed, and work was being done on the preservation of older buildings, a task that continues to this day. The local citizens modernized the furniture factory and enlarged the meat and dairy center, creating 25,000 new jobs. Not so long ago the town water plant supplied water for only nine streets, and there were no sewer facilities. Today, with the help of the government, the whole town has water and sewage facilities, and all roads have been newly paved with asphalt. Since 1970, five new schools have been built and a branch of Lublin University has been established in Zamosc. A large cultural center has also been erected, and behind the town on the Lobunka River a seventy-five acre recreation park has been created for the amusement of the rapidly growing population.

At the conspicuously clean station a ticket girl in a blue uniform arranged tickets and seating for us. I struck up a conversation with her and discovered her hobby was collecting printed materials on railroads which she then pasted in scrapbooks. She went to the office and returned with a scrapbook bound in green canvas and enthusiastically showed it to me. On the first page I noticed a clipping of a poem written by Adam Wazyk about a railroad worker:

Impatient with its illumination, kissed
not sufficiently with its own feeling
the locomotive hissed
over the girl, who was kneeling.
Someone, who in passing had seen
a pagan profile of a girl
swore she prayed to a machine
watching her lips curl.
Pouring the prescribed portion of oil
her heart had room;
annointed, she lit the parable
and held the world in her womb.

The last word of this poem fused with the sound of the oncoming train, and we quickly boarded. We asked the conductor for sleeping accommodations for my sick mother, but the only space left on the train, he told us, was his own compartment. To our surprise and gratitude, he gave it to us, even though it was against the railroad's rules. We told him that we had come from America, but he didn't ask us anything about our country. Instead, he talked exclusively of his native Warsaw. He was immensely proud of his reconstructed capital city.

By 1965, Warsaw had been resurrected from complete devastation. Today, almost a million and a half people are living in many new housing projects, and 35,000 students attend fourteen schools of higher education. Almost 2,000 industrial establishments are situated in Warsaw and its environs, and there are thirteen legitimate theaters and opera and concert halls—all of them brand new and packed daily with eager spectators. The part of Warsaw now known as the old city was completely reconstructed from 400-year-old plans in such detail that even the color of the walls has been reproduced exactly. The seventeenth-century column of Zygmunt the Old now stands again in its customary spot. The entire nation worked day and night, winter and summer, to accomplish this miracle. To commemorate this great national effort, Zygmunt Mikulski, a construction laborer, wrote "A Hymn of Building."

And this was the building of a night
(Brand the mark of this night on my mind)
The flared lines of iron rails and tempered timber
Concrete creaking its endless belt in wheeled barrows.
The gonged counterpoint of steel on steel.
Up on the crowning floor
Hands and hands and hands,
Where stronger than song is the embrace of brick and hands.

Perhaps a solitary bicycle rider
Grew his gaze on the crawling wall, as castaway on a straw of
land.
At night most things are put away. And dreams possess the mass of
man. But not here.
For here the dream of betterness is made awake out of bricks
heaped up.
The plumb-line cries skyward up.
The flame stirs a firing passion.
And, made stronger, the poets bind their beings with long night-
awakened words.

Our first stop in Warsaw was the four-story brick hospital building on Nowowiejska Street where, without Blue Cross or Blue Shield and without any other fuss, we registered my mother. The hospital officials didn't inquire if we could pay or not, but promptly gave her a room. While they administered the tests, my family went to the home of my third and last brother. He is in the shipping trade and lives with his wife and two sons in the Muranow District of the capital. I stayed behind, awaiting the medical results, on a bench in the hospital garden.

It was early morning and the sparrows descended in flutter-ing clusters with loud, sharp calls in search of food. Nurses scurried between buildings, in and out of doorways, mingling with uniformed doctors, stethoscopes jostling about their collars. I was tired and started dozing. The sounds of footsteps mingled with the chirpings of sparrows, and as I blinked I saw the birds walking around my feet. Soon I heard heavy footsteps approaching.

As I opened my eyes, I saw first a pair of brown shoes, then sleepily raising my head, white trousers, white jacket, and an outstretched hand. Before I had focused all these impressions, I heard a man's voice saying, "Good morning."

"Marek? Marek!"

"Yes," he said, smiling gently.

"After so many years . . ." I was back to my youth before the war and words would not come.

He started the conversation. "Your mother is not doing too well."

"What's wrong with her?"

"There's some problem with her heart, one kidney is malfunctioning, and she has a rash on her body of unknown origin. She also has terrible varicose veins on both legs, which should be operated on immediately."

"Is there any hope of curing her?"

"When a man is alive there is always hope. Anyway, your mother will have the best care possible here."

Knowing Marek, I felt confident that my mother was in excellent hands. After we finished conversing, I went to see her. Her room was large by hospital standards and very clean. A vase of freshly cut flowers stood on the dresser. I stayed for a while, assuring her that everything would be all right.

And everything did turn out all right. Today my mother is physically quite well considering she is a woman of eighty-three. She is not interested in television and lives mostly in the past. Whenever I come to Poland, she, together with my three brothers, visits my father's grave. She never asks our wives or our children to accompany us, perhaps because she wants things to be as they were so many years ago when I left Poland. She still cooks on her own little stove. She prefers it this way, she says, because she is no longer able to eat as my farmer brother and his family do. But on birthdays and holidays she joins them for a meal and always manages to find the right moment to sing my father's favorite song, "Mountaineer, Are You Not Lonesome for Your Country?" My father had a strong bass voice much like that of the Russian singer

Fyodor Chaliapin. He was fond of this song about the mountaineer who had left Poland to search for work to support his family and longed to return home. My father has now been dead some twenty years.

My mother remains meticulous about her appearance, spending a half hour each day carefully combing and braiding her long hair that is still streaked with black. Most of her time is spent in keeping her living space in immaculate order and preparing for her next journey to my father's grave site.

When I left the hospital and reached the street, I immediately recognized the scent of red brick, cement, and flowers. Looking down the street, I could see rows and rows of flowers in the distance. Flowers in rich reds, yellows, and blues were planted in window boxes on the balconies of most of the houses.

Later, I learned the importance of flowers to the Polish people. This occurred when we were invited to a name's day celebration, which takes the place of birthdays in Poland. It was St. Anne's day, and we decided to buy flowers as a gift for Anka Pianowski, the wife of a historian friend of mine. We hailed a taxi and asked the driver to take us to the nearest florist.

He first said, "Impossible, impossible today in Warsaw. Perhaps a drive to the country where you can pick your own."

His advice seemed so absurd that we asked him to take us to a florist anyway. He transported us from one florist to another. No roses. No carnations. No flowers of any kind. We bought candy instead. As I found out, in Poland people bring flowers when they visit, and Anne is a very popular name.

My first observations of the city people, especially the women, convinced me that they knew how to dress; they wore both domestic and foreign cloth, made into ingenious styles. As in New York the taxi drivers were alert and very talkative, but not as expensive: ten dollars of New York time and distance for less than a dollar. On my way from the hospital to the heart of the Muranow District and my brother's apartment, I had no sooner stepped into the cab than the driver noticed that I was an American. So he began the following story: "I was leaving home this morning and my five-year-old son said to me, 'Buy me a car.' And I told him sadly, 'When you grow up, you will buy yourself a car.' To this my son said, 'Papa, you are big—why are you driving a state car? Why don't you have your own?' "

I interrupted the driver, "Don't worry. You'll get your tip, but not such a tip as to buy yourself a car! As you can see, I am also grown up."

"Please forgive me, but I'm not telling you my story about my little Rysio to get a big tip from you, really."

"All right, I believe you," I said, not really convinced at all.

"Please do! Look, I'll tell you another story about my son. Yesterday my wife, myself, Rysio, and the younger one, Zbysio, who is only three years old, were invited for supper to my mother-in-law's house. Zbysio took such a long time to get dressed that my Rysio said to me, 'Why do we always have to wait for him? Any place we go we always have to wait for him. He's never ready.' So I said to him, 'He is small and doesn't know how to dress himself any faster. And you know how it is with young children.' But Rysio asked me, 'Why is he younger?' I became exasperated and said, 'Because he was born later.' And then Rysio said, 'You see, he's always late. He was even born later.' "

The taxi driver started laughing loudly and I laughed right along. When we got to Dzierzynski Place, the driver said, "Before the war this was called Bank Place. For the last hundred years it was the scene of many demonstrations by Warsaw workers against foreign and domestic oppression. Behind those buildings over there, behind the Dzierzynski Monument, are the offices of the Warsaw National Council."

We then drove past the city center, and he pointed out a new building complex. "This is our party building, which was built through a collection from all our brothers. My labor and my brick are there too."

We had now come to Constitution Plaza, which is the center of Marszalkowska, a place with huge apartment projects with trees, courtyards, and playgrounds. When I noticed stores with large picture windows full of a variety of goods, I asked him to stop for a minute so that I could do some shopping.

"Oh, not here," he said, "it's much better in Cepelia. That's the center for all kinds of handicraft work."

"I'm tired and can't appreciate all these things right now. I would just like to buy some Polish whiskey, cold cuts, bread, fruit, perhaps some pastry, and go to my brother's place to have a meal and fall asleep." He agreed, telling me he would, of course, take me to where I could do the shopping. But before we drove from this spot, he said, "You'll eat and sleep much better if you see just two things first."

"And what are they?"

"Our Palace of Culture, the W–Z Highway, and. . .

"What's the W–Z Highway?"

"That's the road which runs from east to west, cutting Warsaw into two parts. On both sides of it you can find many beautiful buildings covering total destruction."

"My eyes are closing. In the past three days I have been looking and listening so much my head is spinning."

"All right, we will go straight to Mila Street," he concluded in firm resignation as he skillfully maneuvered the cab in the traffic. For the next five minutes we traveled in silence until I noticed a towering off-white building.

"What's that?"

"The Palace of Culture. It has 3,200 rooms, 40 of which house scientific and cultural institutions. Do you like the building?"

"Surrounded by the smaller buildings and all the trees in the background, it looks almost majestic."

"Some people don't like it, but I do. Very much actually. You see, we got this palace as a gift from the people of the Soviet Union."

"So why don't they like it if they got it free?"

"Let's change the subject. Can I tell you a story—not about my sons?"

"Please do. I hope you are not angry at me because of my comments."

"Oh, I've already forgotten about them. But the story goes this way: One day an American met a Pole on the top floor of the

Palace. The Pole was looking through a pair of binoculars. The American asked him, 'What are you looking at?'

"'I am looking for better times,' replied the Pole.

"'Tell me, how much do you get for doing this?'

"'Five thousand *zyoltys* a month.'

"'Not bad. Not bad at all. But in America you can get twice that amount and in dollars too. Wouldn't you like to come to America?'

"'I'd have to ask my wife.'

"Next day the American met the Pole in the same place. 'Are you coming with me to the United States?'

"'No!' replied the Pole, continuing to look through the binoculars.

"'And why not?' asked the puzzled American.

"'I am an old man. If I lost my job in America, I'd starve to death because nobody would give an old man a job.'

"'You'll grow old here too.'

"'And here, sir, the government has to give me a job. If not, they at least have to support me and my family. That is the law.'"

We traveled down narrow streets bordered by trees planted in orderly patterns. Then the taxi turned left and we were in a square in the middle of which stood a monument. I looked at the massive granite blocks covered with a powerfully sculptured bas-relief. The taxi driver observed, "This is the monument dedicated to the war heroes of the Warsaw ghetto. It stands in eternal remembrance of the 1943 Warsaw uprising when 50,000 Jews lost their lives in one of the epic battles of the Second World War."

I got out of the taxi to look around. The huge blocks were carved with many figures of men and women prepared to fight German fascists. Fresh flowers surrounded the monument, and a group of young people from a foreign country was taking photographs. Behind this monument, sculptured by Natan Rappaport, were the ruins of a building untouched since the war. Together with the monument, the ruins excited an immediate feeling of horror and compassion for the sufferings of the Jewish people.

Not far from us now was Mila Street, my final destination.

My driver helped carry my packages to the second floor of the apartment building where my brother Marion lived. For this courtesy I gave him 200 *zlotys* and a bag of candies. I greeted my brother who had spent four years in a Nazi concentration camp, and we both started crying. Under the pretext of making lunch, our wives shooed the children outside.

Marion, his wife Lucyna, and their sons Romek and Ryszek lived in a good-sized four-room apartment, complete with modern facilities. They also had a balcony on which they could sleep during the summer months with no fear of rape or robbery. In the summer, the balcony is covered with pots of geraniums, lilies, and purple-colored flowers. For all this, including gas and electricity, they paid only 400 *zlotys* per month, approximately twelve dollars at the official rate of exchange. My brother, who then worked in the Ministry of Railroads and is a specialist in containerization, and his wife, who worked for the state radio, made a combined salary of close to 6,000 *zlotys* a month.

In the four-story building where they lived, as in almost all other buildings in the big cities, the tenants had many different occupations. There were workers, scientists, civil employees, and journalists who rented apartments on the basis of family size. The building was spotless. It had very wide stairs and no elevator. Three other buildings of similar size and construction surrounded a courtyard, open on all four sides in which flowers and shrubs grew. Such projects are immaculate—no garbage, no broken glass, no dog droppings. In all the times I have been in Poland since 1963, I have never heard, nor even seen, a fire engine, much less any fires. I have also witnessed two dog fights, but no other kinds of fighting.

In the middle of my brother's courtyard there were four sandboxes, four swings, and other playground equipment. Children are quite literally at the center of this life. They normally spend their time after school acting out life in this courtyard until dinnertime. After their meals it is homework time.

Later that day, when we went down to the courtyard there were children playing. I approached one nine-year-old boy and asked him who was his greatest hero. He said, "The unknown soldier."

"What would you like to be in your life?"

"An electrical engineer."

I found this practical response to be typical of these children. While they dreamed of idealistic ventures, they thought of themselves and their future in realistic terms.

Gloria quickly found young playmates in the courtyard and taught them the games of marbles and jacks. In turn, the Polish children taught her their dodge-ball game. By this time both Gloria and Anthony could converse in Polish on a simple level.

With the school year practically ended and final examinations in progress, the younger schoolgoers anxiously awaited their vacation. The parents, too, were planning their vacations—one year it would be a camp by the Baltic Sea, the next year a journey through the Carpathian Mountains, and another year a stay on a farm or in a state forest. Normally, the Poles have four-week vacations. The state, as well as some of the union organizations, support the vacation areas set aside for young people at a cost of over one billion *zlotys* a year. If the youngsters can't leave their parents' home, a so-called day vacation is organized by the Scouts' Society, the Association of Children's Friends, or various factories and offices. Every morning recreation guides pick up the children and take them by bus on outings to various sites where they eat lunch and play before returning home in the evening. Teenagers, though, enjoy spending their time traveling throughout the country and learning about historical sights under the guidance of trained adults.

After resting, I received a phone call from the poet Leon Pasternak, with whom I had an appointment at the Bolero Bar. From there he brought my wife and me to his home, where he introduced us to his old Hungarian wine and his new, young wife. When I asked him what had happened to his first wife, he replied after scratching his bald head, "One day my wife said to me, 'When I get old I am going to put a bullet through my head.' So I said to her, 'Fire!'"

After we left the Pasternaks my wife and I visited the Writers Café, where we met the satirist Jozef Prutkowski and his friend, the painter Ignacy Witz, a short, dark-haired man with a bushy mustache. During our conversation they managed to tear apart all the arts and make fun of just about everybody, except, of course, themselves. Perhaps this critical approach to art and life kept them in their prominent positions. When we left the café, I said to Sophia, "There is nothing new under the sun," and I tried hard to recall the name of the Egyptian pharoah who said that to be the master over people you must criticize them until they are afraid to act.

That evening, on our way to the state opera to see *Swan Lake*, we saw night life in Warsaw for the first time. There were not many colorful displays but plenty of people were rushing off to theaters, movies, restaurants, and cafés. The production of *Swan Lake* was excellent with a well-trained troupe who danced in the style of the Russian school. The house was packed and responded very enthusiastically. Next to me, in the fourth row, sat an old farmer clapping so hard that his wife kept grabbing at his hands to stop him. In Poland, not only are folk dancing and the classics like *Swan Lake* stressed as in the Soviet Union, but other dance forms as well. In fact, the Polish Dance Theater, currently under the inventive direction of Conrad Drzewiecki, is as wideranging in its offerings and styles as any dance company in the world. Ballets which Drzewiecki has choreographed have been set to the music of the English Renaissance composers as well as to that of Handel, Bartok, Stravinsky, and Duke Ellington. They are contemporary and exciting sensual experiences.

The next day was Sunday. My family went for a walk through the streets of Warsaw while I took the suburban railroad to the town of Siedlce to visit an old friend, who I learned was spending his second year in jail for "negligence" connected with buying and selling. When I got off at the station, I went to a nearby store to buy some fruit, cheese, and candy. I decided to walk to the jail. On the street I met a group of people dressed in their best clothing, who were either going to or coming from church and talking incessantly. When they saw that my walk was leading to the jail, they started to point at me. I could read in their eyes, "Why are you here? Where are you going? How many years?" I hurried briskly through the brown wooden gates; a guard asked me to go to the waiting room. He went into another room, presumably to report my presence. Immediately I noticed four things—quiet, distinct coolness coming from the thick walls (it was summertime and therefore really noticeable), meticulous order and cleanliness, and the pastel-painted walls.

The guard came and took me to a different building. I observed that the prisoners were dressed in civilian clothing. Everybody, including the guards, moved slowly, silently, and with severe looks on their faces. I approached one of the prisoners and said, "Good morning."

"Good morning," he replied with a smile on his round face.

"And what is your reason for being here?"

"One reason is that I freely participated in weddings."

"You mean you sit in jail in a socialist country for participating in weddings?"

"Yes," he replied with sadness in his voice, "every time I went to these weddings I was the groom."

"And how many years did you get?"

"Five."

"Five years for being a bigamist? That's too much, no?"

"Not exactly; in addition I had a conversation with the judge."

"What kind of conversation?"

"Oh, the judge asked me, after my last marriage, why I had robbed the same store three times. And I told him that I was very much in love with my wife. The judge was puzzled. I figured that his feelings towards me might be softened if I told him that, so I added an explanation: 'The first time I went was to pick up a few dresses for my wife. And the other times I went to exchange them because she didn't care for the colors!'"

I met my friend, as one would meet in an office or hotel lobby. We sat on wooden chairs at a square table in a room decorated with some paintings of village scenes by Polish artists. We talked of personal matters and current events in international politics. As one of the guards was passing in the corridor, my friend asked him to come in and join our conversation. From the guard I learned that many different types of prisoners were housed in this jail and that they could choose to work in the fields or in the various shops and offices. Emphasis was placed on mental rehabilitation and political education, for which all kinds of lecturers and discussions were provided—some even led by specialists in the field. I also detected a friendliness between the jailed and the jailers, which was strengthened by their common enemy—the monotony of daily routine. To pass the time, some of the prisoners played chess or painted Christmas cards. When I thought of jails in other countries, I had to conclude that Polish jails compared very favorably. A guard told me that when people are not satisfied with existing conditions, progress can usually be made. He added that if the people on the outside liked jails as well as the people on the inside, there would no longer be any need to continue building them.

The war, especially the indiscriminate killing of the civilian population by the fascist occupiers, had a negative effect on the moral outlook of the Polish people. After it was over, the Polish government had great difficulty in coping with indigenous criminal acts. Sometimes they used, *per fas et nefas*, physical force. But today there is peace, as the contemporary poet Jan Huszcza can vouch.

Peace is present: scythes on the grasses sigh.
Agile ponies tender their snorts as they come.
Village on village blows wreaths from bustling fires.
Factories pipe to the skies and the sidewalks hum.
While girl upon girl tricks a flower in her hair a-sly.

Peace is present: rivers tumble great wheels
And glitter gay lights in the evening windows.
In the ripening woods the sweet wild raspberry reels,
And calls from bed of hidden leaf-made pillows.
While chortling mills grind up a people's meal.

Peace is present: silver birches in the hills
Sing greening songs while swinging the sunlight about.
The stone teaches the sculptor, flints his will.
School bells tumble the houses inside out.
And man for man a friendliness is sealed.

Upon returning from my visit to the jail, my wife informed me that during the day we had received several telephone calls and three dinner invitations. We accepted an invitation from Andrzej and Karolina Jus, both prominent psychiatrists. They lived in Wyzwolenia Alley in a four-room apartment with mahogany furniture and many paintings. The supper was casual and the conversation soon turned to Polish medicine. Andrzej was the director of the Psychiatric Clinic of the Academy of Medicine in Warsaw. Karolina's specialty was child psychology; at the moment she was doing research in retrograde amnesia. Andrzej told me, "In Poland the tradition of psychiatric care is very old. It goes back to the Middle Ages. The very first Polish collection of written law, the so-called Statute of Wislica, introduced in 1347 by King Casimir the Great, contains a short reference to psychiatric care. The law made the families of the mentally ill and the communal authorities responsible for caring for the insane."

Karolina added, "Later, psychiatric care was concentrated in special asylums and hospitals for mentally ill patients. The first hospitals of this kind were founded in the sixteenth century in Cracow, Gdansk, and, in the seventeenth century, in Warsaw and Wilno."

"And what are your plans for the future?" my wife asked. "I suppose the war experience has increased mental illness."

Andrzej replied. "Yes, it has. But since Poland was able to stabilize herself and is now flourishing, mental illness resulting from social stress has abated considerably. We can now concentrate our efforts on more subtle forms of mental illness and do pioneer work in the field. Psychiatric work is coordinated by the Department for the Diseases of the Nervous System in the Ministry of Health and Social Welfare. This department is also charged with creating new environments for the mentally ill that include day and night hospitals, clubs, and family assistance. Educational facilities have been enlarged to train psychologists, social workers, psychiatric nurses, and occupational therapists."

Karolina, who has no children of her own and has spent her life working with them, added, "Special attention is being given to the development of child psychiatry. The number of foreign fellowships for all psychiatrists has been increased. Poland is receiving assistance in this area from the World Health Organization and from different foundations which provide a certain number of foreign fellowships for the education of Polish psychiatrists. Special fellowships are being given to young psychiatric research workers."

From our conversation I learned that Poland has made great advances in the treatment of mental diseases. More immediately, this has translated itself into less isolation of the mentally ill from the rest of society through treatment in out-patient departments or in psychiatric wards in general hospitals and a larger resocialization program for the discharged patients. The best treatment for unhealthy people, as the nation has found, is to introduce them to a healthy society in new roles.

Chapter 8

the plains rise
on the wild bird
whirring
across the sky our chargers plunge foamed breath
outstreaming
the hedges woke
the vibrant thicket spins
where butterflies newstirring clop the miraculous night
with rainbowed wings

> on heavenly steeds we gallop
> stables on cloud behind us
> stallions of heaven our mounts

no inns shall
harbor us
no crosses threaten
who see but our own hearts in this sweet sod
nor grope
for better faith
that this togetherness
wherein belief has scope sufficing

> what matters earth
> what matter men
> for us what heaven

outrunning time we are ourselves infinity
who with your love allreaching from two beings
take
beauty
to make
        divinity

Later in the evening, Anthony joined us at a cafe where I was to meet some old friends. I approached my reunion with some trepidation, for after many years' absence it is always difficult to talk with those who have shared your youth in the shadow of great desire. One just doesn't know what to expect.

When we arrived I saw the poet Adam Wazyk and Jerzy Jasienski, the former director of the *Teatr Polski*. Adam, short and then in his late sixties, had more the look of an owner of a grocery store than an artist. This impression was dispelled when he began talking. He immediately leaped into conversation, but instead of arguing American politics, as he had expected, to his delight I asked him to recite his poem "Sunday" from his larger work *Semaphores*. Putting aside his briefcase which he carries with him day and night, he sipped some coffee, stared into the dim lights, and began:

During the day out of town on the river which has taken off her
*   petticoats of foam*
Seagulls are toy boats and white sails with noise coming from
*   everywhere.*
You are swallowing cream of the skies on the out skirts of a town on
*   the banks of the river in greens,*
Jostling as hips of the blossoming girls.
During the night (when the bridge appears), immediately the lamp
Asking for the grace of caressing the street.
Bare flesh of light coming and going:
You want to kiss with your lips and stroke with your hands.

Comforting and touching-soft as plush
The night is like a girl trembling
And your heart as dynamite in your chest
But you are afraid of the flesh because tonight even the
*   dark is shining.*

Already arteries are throbbing
And love gives your lips soft road
Traveling to where two eyes more piercing than searchlights
Go through you with prongs of love.

I next turned to Jerzy Jasienski, an excellent pianist and a great lover of French, Russian, and Polish poetry. For many years he had organized international musical competitions; he was concentrating on national artistic events. Jerzy wore very thick glasses on a big nose and was a more polished man than Adam. (Later in our stay, he helped us by securing many social invitations from theatrical and film people. I was at a loss as to why he had been so generous. Sophia volunteered the explanation: "It's because his nose and yours are so similar that you could be brothers.")

That night we met a number of other people prominent in the arts. We talked with Dr. Ludwik Kasinski, the head of the state publishing house Czytelnik, which is responsible for bringing many American books to Polish readers. Novelist Roman Bratny, who was to leave the following day on a freighter bound for Boston, spent most of the evening discussing American fiction with my son Anthony. Mieczyslaw Jastrun, whose poetry I had read some time ago in French translation and who was on his way to the resort town of Zakopane, talked with my wife at length. In another corner I had a long discussion with Jastrun's wife about the American children's books which she was writing under the name of Mieczyslawa Buczkowna.

The next day we traveled around the city with the renowned Polish cartoonist and painter Karol Ferster. Karol amused us with a personal identification card which he always carried with him:

Last name—F.
First name—K.
Pseudonym—Charlie
Present occupation—Artist
Occupation for which you are trained—Lawyer
Forbidden Occupation—Violinist
Age—Second Youth
Height—Shrimp
Eyes—One is twinkling
Hair color—I don't remember
Marks—A number on the arm, the Nazi keys of death
Greatest Achievement—Living

One of the areas Karol drove us to in his car was a place under the Poniatowski Bridge where people trade and sell used cars. Aside from hundreds of potential buyers, sellers, and onlookers, we saw gamblers playing dice and cards and vendors selling fruits and flowers. This area is legally designated for car-selling and allows the owner of the vehicle a spot to exhibit his auto for a fee of 100 *zlotys*. If the owner succeeds in selling his car, he must pay the government 3 percent of the sale price. As I soon discovered, cars that are sold here often come by strange routes. Among the sellers was a stocky man with straggly hair who was standing beside an old Ford with a smashed-in front. I asked him how his car was damaged.

"Two Sundays ago my wife went for a drive. When she returned, I asked her, 'Where's the car?' And she told me, 'Partly in the garage.' So you see, sir, part of the car is damaged, and I am selling just two-thirds of my Ford, which I have dragged here under the bridge."

Upon further reflection, he looked at me and then at his car and concluded, "If somebody, not you, is a good mechanic, he can fix it."

Karol next took us to the Palace of Culture. At the building's entrance stand two monuments, one of the Polish astronomer Nicholas Copernicus and the other of the poet Adam Mickiewicz. An elevator brought us rapidly to the thirteenth floor, where Karol asked us to tell him what we saw.

"Naturally, a panorama of Warsaw," I said with a trace of irritation in my voice.

"Don't think me foolish for asking the obvious," Karol countered. "I have to tell you that this is the most beautiful view in the world."

"I have seen many beautiful places and I don't think this is the most beautiful in the world."

"Oh, but it is. Because from here you can see the capital and not this ugly palace."

Karol told me that many Poles routinely play this joke on foreigners to show their annoyance at the fact that the highest building in Warsaw was a gift from Stalin. Later in our visit

we returned with the children to this Soviet memorial to
Warsaw to see *Samuel Zborowski*, a play written by Juliusz
Slowacki. It made a tremendous impression on us, even though
Sophia and the children had difficulty with the language.

Half of the drama takes place in an unidentified mountain area
in nineteenth-century Poland, and the other half in an imaginary
fairyland. Seen from a mythological perspective, the drama offers
interesting ideas on the poetic manifestation of fantasy in one's
private, spiritual life and on its importance in society's overall life.
The work can also be viewed as a political drama. Especially in its
second part, it gives insight into the twentieth-century's moral
sensibility and its concern with justice. The brilliant staging of this
fusion of mythological imagery and social and artistic realism
fascinated us and inspired a genuine respect for contemporary
Polish theater.

Our admiration of Polish theater must not be unique, for
Warsaw's score of beautiful new theaters are attended by millions
every year. In Poland culture is for everyone, and as prices for the
best seats in the house are less than a dollar, everyone can afford to
patronize the theaters. On our trip in 1963 I also saw Wladyslaw
Krzeminski's brilliantly staged production of Camus's *Caligula*.
Seated in front of me in the eighth row, orchestra center, was a
peasant and his wife, both of whom displayed an evident appreciation for what was occurring on stage.

If you are feeling romantic, as I was the night we saw *Samuel
Zborowski*, you can go anywhere in Warsaw in a horsedrawn
carriage. The city also offers public transportation on trolleys or
buses which are run on the honor code. The tickets are sold in a
kiosk, and the vehicle contains a machine that punches your ticket
which then becomes your receipt. Checkers board the buses at
random to see if everyone has purchased a ticket. Those who have
no tickets are not arrested, but publicly admonished. The ensuing
embarrassment is considered sufficient punishment.

My friend Karol prides himself on his knowledge of Warsaw.
He maintains that the name *Warszawa* (Warsaw) does not come
from "wars" and "sawa," but rather from the name of its first
citizen, Warsz. This is only his own theory.

Another of our excursions with Karol took us to Lazien-kowski Park. The park has a palace on a lake which is one of the finest examples of classical Polish architecture. In this palace Poland's last Polish king, Stanislaw August Poniatowski, gave a dinner every Thursday to which he invited the outstanding artists and scientists of Europe. Today the well-kept park (all of Poland's parks are well-kept, lush with vegetation, and completely safe) serves as a recreation center for public activity. It also has two beautiful monuments to Fryderyk Chopin and Prince Jozef Poniatowski and architectural landmarks, such as the Hunters' Palace, the Theater on the Island, the White House, and the Orange Building.

During our visit to the Orange Building, an exhibition of works of 150 painters, 30 sculptors, and 40 graphic artists was being held. A piece of sculpture in rock entitled *A Child's Head*, by Wiktoria Wysocka, impressed my wife very much. Anthony, who is interested in astronomy, was naturally captivated by a sculpture in wood, *The Dead Meteors,* by Wlodzimierz Now-akowski. The strong *Portrait of the Polish Scientist*, done in bronze by Alfons Karny, struck me by the beauty of its lines. Gloria was fascinated by color lithography such as *Summer* by Maria Schwartz-Schier and *Sisters* worked in ink by Tadeusz Kobylka. Oil paintings by such artists as Jonasz Stern, Marian Warzecha, Tadeusz Kantor, Jan Tarasin, and Rejmund Ziemski, to mention only a few, express the different technical approaches through which these Polish artists assert themselves in the Euro-pean market. Warzecha, who was represented in 1960 at the Museum of Modern Art in New York and has organized his own school of painters in Poland, and Ziemski with his moody land-scapes impressed me very much. Others such as Zbigniew Makowski and Tarasin were highly ornamental and colorful. *Two Girls*, painted by Kazimierz Mikulski, is cleverly designed and makes abundant use of color; and the compositions of Adam Marczynski possess the characteristic of precision in craftsman-ship. Although I didn't like *Spring in Raszyn*, painted by Wawrzyniec Chorembalski, I admired the artist as a man. He was short, bald, and dressed in green trousers and held a blue hat in his hand; he charmed me with his conversation about "the old Warsaw."

Karol then led us to an American-style supermarket aptly called "Super Sam" where we bought smoked fish, ham, Polish cheeses, and fruit. From there we drove to Kanonia Street, a very picturesque part of "the old Warsaw" which has been restored completely, even down to the bright fine details of the pavement. The government has donated these beautiful old homes to the artists so that they may concentrate on painting without worry over eviction for nonpayment of rent.

Next, we visited the realist painter, Aleksander Rafalowski, who lives in Warsaw with his charming wife in security, peace, and fame. He fashions oil still lifes from very simple elements: gray seashells, artisans' tools, fish bones and skin, lamps, old photographs, broken brushes, plates, and used cloth. He presents these objects in quiet, subdued arrangements. It seemed to me that the predominating color gray successfully represented the poetry of one's daily life. During the war, he lost 300 of his paintings and 2,000 drawings in the fire storm that incinerated the city. Although he is now in his late seventies, he still works daily, steadily laying down huge compositions of contrasting color and form, while his wife arranges his exhibitions throughout Europe. During our warm conversation he presented us with one of his still lifes. Later, when we returned to America, we learned that he regretted this presentation, for he considered it to be one of his best efforts.

Our day closed with a visit to the Classic Theater to see Jean Giraudoux's *La Guerre de Troie n' aura pas Lieu* (*There Will Be No Trojan War*). Andromeda was played masterfully by Aleksandra Karzynska; Helena Norowicz in the role of Cassandra and Zygmunt Kestowicz as Hector were also very effective. The play was under the excellent direction of Jerzy Kaliszewski.

Later, I saw on stage actors such as Gustaw Holoubek in *A Midsummer Night's Dream*, Ms. Z. Mrozowska in Oscar Wilde's *A Florentine Tragedy*, Tadeusz Lomnicki in the title role of Bertold Brecht's *The Rise of Arturo Ui*, and J. Woszczerowicz in the title role of Shakespeare's *Richard III*. Such fine actors and productions are comparable to those found in New York, Paris, or London. I was astounded by the vitality of Polish theater.

In most cities, however, movie houses outnumber live theaters and draw proportionately larger audiences. The cinematic tradition in Poland began with the first experiments that led to a mechanical box showing moving pictures. In the 1890s, Piotr Lebiedzinski feverishly sought to produce a camera that would make photographs come alive. Once he and others working independently of him accomplished this task, the cinema arts rapidly assumed an important place in Polish life. In the period between the two world wars, Polish film production proliferated as film makers transposed great literature onto the screen.

After Poland's liberation from the Nazis, film production and distribution were freed to reflect the needs of the socialist state. The war had been such a shattering experience that, for the first decade or so, directors concentrated on expressing their feelings on it. *The Last Stop* (1948), directed by Wanda Jakubowska, a Dantean tragedy about a Nazi extermination camp, and *Border Street* (1949), directed by Aleksander Ford, also about resistance to Nazi horror, are masterpieces of this genre. However, in the early postwar years producers so interfered with directors that only a few quality films were produced.

With the change in power from Bierut to Gomulka, Poland's film industry became more creative. Artistic currents from both East and West were combined with the directors' war experiences to form the Polish School. In the films produced by this School, war was no longer glorified as it had been in the high-flying historical epics of the prewar years. It was not portrayed realistically as the terrifying machine that devours men. Characters went to their doom in full recognition that their deaths would not bring salvation to others. Such directors as Wajda, Munk, Has, and Kawalerowicz transformed the past into a grim absurdity.

The great films of the Polish School include *Canal* and *Ashes and Diamonds*, both directed by Andrzej Wajda. Made in 1957, *Canal* has been sold to 50 countries and, as such, has been Poland's most popular film export. The sale of her films abroad undoubtedly brings more hard currency to Poland's treasury than even the Polish ham that is sold the world over.

In *Canal*, the entire film takes place underground during the war in the bleak stench of Warsaw's sewers hemmed in by barbed wire and mines. Whenever some insurgents manage to escape, they are cut down by German soldiers who occupy what little light exists.

Ashes and Diamonds draws a complex portrait of a doomed member of the right in the underground. By holding on to the values of the past that oppressed the Polish masses, he is trapped in a meaningless struggle.

Counterpoint to Wajda's romantic fatalism are the films by director Kazimierz Kutz, *Salt of the Black Earth* (1970) and *The Pearl in the Crown* (1972). Both center on those Poles who prove that struggle and resistance can indeed lead to progress. In these films, the Pole is no longer merely a plaything of history. He is now the master of his own destiny, resisting and fighting back. His efforts are not in vain, even if he suffers death in the process.

By the 1960s, the war had become the experience of those old enough to remember it and was no longer of immediate interest. The newer generation is more concerned with the social disloca-tion caused by migrations from the country to the city. The problems of adjustment associated with this move form the theme of Wojciech Has's richly textured character portraits in his film *Gold* (1962).

The difficulties of youth undergoing socialization are taken up in Henryk Kluba's *Skinny and Others* (1968) and Jerzy Skolimowski's *Identification Marks—None* (1964).

Reflecting the interest of the newer generation, Poland's contemporary directors are now dealing with the individual's problems in coping with a society undergoing rapid transfor-mation, rather than with the individual's sacrifice to preserve or further national existence. Individual needs and psycholog-ical universals are being examined. Lenartowicz's *Red and Gold* (1970) deals gracefully with the problems of aging, while Slesicki's *Moving Sands* (1969) mingles nature and youth to create a moving film of subtle lyricism.

In *Deluge* (1974), we have the monumental achievement of young director Jerzy Hoffman who, in dealing with the sixteenth-century invasion of Poland by Sweden, presents all the newer elements of individualization in the traditional epic form. His work represents the most complete depiction of the faces and forces that have shaped the Polish past.

Chapter 9

From crimespun lotteries of thought
he came
gave free his simple text of brotherhood
and lacerated
        died
that future pharisees might trade
upon his name
yet nones to blame
he is
the agelong victim
        of
           mankind

While in Poland, we generally stayed in private houses rather than in hotels. Even so, we were required to notify the authorities about our addresses. Before we left the United States, we had filled out forms indicating that we would be staying in my mother's village home, but as our time there had been cut short, we stayed, with my brother in Warsaw. When I went to Mostowski Palace to register my family, the clerk insisted that I also continue to register a few hundred miles away at my mother's village. In my old-fashioned direct Polish way, I told him that it was stupid to have to register in a place where I was not living, and I wagered him a bottle of Polish brandy that ultimately I would not be forced to do so. The clerk agreed to the wager, and in a surge of generosity I also added taxi fare to the main police station where I was going to argue my case.

"Good," he said, and he called a taxi.

The station was on the other side of the city. As I rode, I decided I would debate the regulations with the first official I spotted. When I arrived, a tall young man with a dozen or so pencils in his breast pocket was the first person I saw, and he whisked me into his office.

"And who informed you that you'd have to travel a few hundred miles to register?" he asked.

Sitting down in the chair he had offered me, trying to catch my breath, I stated in exasperation that I had just come from Mostowski Palace where the fellow in charge had told me so.

"Rubbish!" he said. Stretching one hand out, he asked me for my passport, and with his other hand he fingered his pencils. He left with my passport, and before I could scratch my head, he had returned. "Do you remember the name of the official who didn't want to register you?" he asked as he returned my passport.

No longer irritated now that I had held my own against bureaucrats, I responded quietly that I didn't.

Outside in the corridor I met a woman whom I recognized, Zosia En. Although I hadn't seen her for decades, she looked as if time had not touched her. Her dark hair, big brown eyes, and full lips all came back to me; her walk was still energetic. She was the sister of a university colleague whom I didn't want to contact, because, quite frankly, I wasn't sure if he would remember me. He now held an important government position.

After the usual amenities which are spoken when meeting someone from the distant past, I broke the banality of our conversation: "No ill will intended, but I recall you always wanted to be a policewoman, and if I am not mistaken you have succeeded."

"I'm not a policewoman, just a teacher who happens to work in this building." She smiled, revealing a gold crown on one of her teeth.

"I know that your brother wanted to be a politician or a writer. I know he is the first, though probably he is longing to be the second."

"Have you called him?"

"No."

"And why not?"

"Do you think that after so many years an ordinary man with an ordinary passport can call on a man who not only has a different color but also a different type of passport?"

"Fairy tales. You were always good at fairy tales."

"Yes, I know. And Klara. How is Klara, your sister-in-law? Did she find her place in life?"

"You mean the theater?"

"Yes, she was always in love with the theater."

"Klara is working in the Ministry of Culture. She is in charge of a very important theater."

"Well, faith will find its way."

My wife and I spent the next three evenings in the hospitable homes of the Ens—three different but related families. First, we visited Klara, who lived on Stepinska Street with her teenaged children (a son, Zbyszek, and a daughter, Krysia). Here I witnessed the strong interest of some Polish youth in domestic and foreign politics. I also discovered that they spent their leisure time in sports and dancing, just as their counterparts in the West. Different from the West, however, was the more active interest of Polish youth in experimental art and science. This interest is encouraged by the many literary, musical, and artistic contests that are held in Poland.

Krysia, a girl with brown hair and of medium height, had striking, inquisitive eyes. She expressed a deep love for literature, especially for the poet Tadeusz Rozewicz, whose poems speak particularly to today's youth. For example:

Be not ashamed of tears
be not ashamed of tears young poets.

Grasp hold of the clichéd moon
the moon-beamed night
true love, the gleaming nightingale.

Be not afraid of heavenly assumption
reach up for the celestial bodies
compare the eyes to the stars.

Move the primrose
with the orange winged butterfly
the rise and descent of the sun.

Pour out peas to the gentle doves
set your smile upon
dogs flowers a rhinoceros and locomotives.

Talk of ideals
declaim an ode to love
confide in the passing stranger.

Naively believe in the beautiful
and with feeling believe in man.

Be not ashamed of tears
be not ashamed of tears young poets.

On the second evening we visited Zosia En, their aunt. Her husband was sick that night and she was very subdued. Our conversation continually returned to him. To our question, "How can we help?" she graciously replied, "We have everything we need. But you, in a strange country, are different. Maybe we can help you see something extra or go to some new place."

My wife answered politely: "Really, that's not necessary.

Everywhere we go, people want to help us—they offer to show us the sights. We just don't have any way to express our appreciation.''

But in spite of Sophia's response, the following evening Zosia took us to the National Theater, a structure built in the eighteenth century and destroyed by the Germans during the war. It has been rebuilt in the same classical style with only two modern improvements: soft, comfortable chairs and air conditioning. That evening we saw a triple bill: Aeschylus's *Agamemnon*, Euripides's *Electra*, and Aristophanes's *The Frogs*, all under the original direction of Kazimierz Dejmek. Although I had seen many different productions of these plays, I was impressed by the harmony of the dialogue and action with the classical style. Anthony, on the other hand, felt that he had discovered something he called "Slavic temperament." He felt that the acting was too emotional for Greek tragedy, even though it was highly intriguing.

Our third evening was spent on Parkowa Street withmy school friend Marion En, his beautiful wife, and their small son. They lived in a comfortable apartment which had oil paintings by Polish masters, an extensive library, and a collection of oriental antiques. For supper we had clear borsch, beefsteak, mushrooms with cream, young potatoes, and asparagus, accompanied by Caucasian red wine; *Gateau hongrois*, coffee, and French brandy completed the meal, with was served graciously on a beautifully set table. The evening was perfect and as socially proper as in diplomatic circles, but with the added warmth of old friendship. We conversed mainly about our respective families and the future of our children. We wondered whether they would live in peace and whether they would be able to develop their talents. Many times Marion returned to talk about our early youth when we had no problems with our studies—only the problem of filling our stomachs. I mentioned his mother, who had been a mother to other boys, feeding and helping them as she would her own sons. Today, these boys are adults; some hold important positions in other parts of the world, and all remember her warm kindness.

As for my own mother, she was still in the hospital on

Nowowiejska Street, and each time I visited her she reminded me of the unattended farm and the chickens she had to get home to feed. After consulting with the doctors, I was able to gain her release. When I inquired about the cost of her hospitalization and medicines, I was told there was no charge. I immediately thought back to a recent occurrence. Only a few weeks before leaving the United States, my father-in-law, who lives on a Social-Security pension in a town just outside of New York City, was required to have an abdominal operation, which cost $2,000. Fortunately, his children were able to raise the sum; otherwise, he would not have had medical attention and could have died.

Mother was driven back to her native village by Bohun Zwolinski, a remarkable man who in his English tweeds looked very much like an English lord. He was employed by the Bureau of Projects and Architectural Studies for Warsaw. His knowledge of the city's buildings and his admiration for different architectural projects seemed almost pathological. He promised to take us to Brwinow to visit Barbara Gordon, a very popular writer of mystery stories, after he returned from taking Mother home. But when he returned, he decided that we must first see Zalew Zegrzynski, a wildlife sanctuary located north of Warsaw, which contains wooded tracts dotted with lakes and a large number of animals and fish, including swans, night herons, and a wide variety of geese and ducks. Through clear lake waters one can spot salmon and catfish. Almost 100,000 acres in size, this territory is covered with linden, oak, pine, jasmine, red currant, dogwood, and sorb trees. It is an ideal site for campers and ordinary visitors, because it has several buildings which can accommodate overnight guests and stores where inexpensive meals or food for the animals can be purchased. Hunting, fishing, and picking flowers are all prohibited.

Unexpectedly, we encountered three writers on contemporary Poland at Zalew Zegrzynski. One was the handsome novelist Wojciech Zukrowski, who was on his way to lecture and vacation in Yugoslavia. The second was Leopold Lewin, a short man of few words but a good poet. The third man was my old friend Jan

Spiewak, whom I had known since early youth. It seemed to me
that he had gotten shorter and had a rounder, perhaps more swollen, face. I learned that he was suffering from a liver ailment; even
so, he was still an optimistic poet. His last poem contains an almost
exact description of the location of our meeting.

*My heart goest out to the swell of the Polish
        lowlands,
The billow of rivers over the plain,
The wheat-bright languid wind-reach of the
        southlands,
The golden harps of grain.*

*The dreaming eager streams, I love, and
        their lust,
And conceiving of flower-dabbed farms,
The dance of the laden branches in house of
        the mist,
And the morning off in its arms.*

*I love the anxieties of breasting fruit
Before the full bursting round.
It is in a shining glance and chest out
That sauce of songs are found.*

*The grass rears up like a violent sea.
A strange dark in each meadow glows.
Surely a storm is free, gleamingly
As the apple tree, or jet of snow.*

*Fish slip to sudden deeps.
The maple crown is flushed and quivers.
A drop falls on the tasting lips
Reeds knock like bells by the rivers.*

The rain, full, feathered and fine,
Will pass obliquely, perversely.
While in the wet of the nested vines
A bird fluffs is feathers free.

A hollow limb knocks.
A cuckoo bird clocks.
A bridge full of a wagon solemnly.
Call out, mother, company.

There the tractor man round and round
Over the stubbled common ground
And the bright mechanic
Cars off at the triple quick.

The green apple tree rushed
With a budding blush.
And the plum tree's
Blue nodding of leaves.

The young cherry bobs on the wind.
The young lover's ride is a kind
Of a song, for the girl at his side
Is good for a coming bride.

The limb knocks along.
The cuckoo clocks on.

When we arrived at Barbara Gordon's home, located in a secluded area of suburban Brwinow, I was struck by the beauty of the birch grove behind her house. These birches were tall, thick, and stately with a slight drooping only at the very top. In contrast, most of the birches I had seen on Long Island were bent out of shape and were blown down before the white bark of youth could peel off. Here in the Gordons' backyard, which resembled a miniature forest, the birches were so high and their foliage so thick that very little sunlight could filter down.

Ms. Gordon's husband was the head of the Jewish Historical Institute, and as such his knowledge of the history and present-day life of Poland's Jews was encyclopedic. The institution he headed serves as the intellectual reservior of power and activity for Jewish life. Its members travel extensively, collecting information on the history of Polish Jews and lecturing and holding scientific seminars in various Jewish universities. These universities are located in Warsaw and in ten other Polish cities, including Lodz, Cracow, Katowice, Wroclaw, Szczecin, Gliwice, and Lignica. The institute publishers two papers, one in Yiddish called *The Historical Papers* and one in Polish called the *Bulletin*.

Despite Poland's small Jewish population, the country retains a lively Jewish cultural life. A large Yiddish publishing house, Yiddish Buch, was organized just after the Second World War and by 1975 had published over two million copies of 400 books on the Jews. The Jewish State Theater, now renamed the Ida Kaminska Theater, puts on new productions, such as *Auschwitz Oratorio* by Alina Nowak, as well as the older classics. The life of the children and teenagers centers around thirty youth clubs; a youth dance club in Wroclaw is one of the best in the country. Jewish drama and chorus circles, together with branches of the Communal and Cultural Federation, exist in many large cities. Approximately 200,000 people attend Jewish theaters and other cultural offerings annually. The newspaper *Folkhtimme*, which is published monthly, is found in practically every Jewish home.

During my 1975 trip, I spoke to the Secretary of the Communal and Cultural Federation of Jews. The first thing I asked him was whether maintaining contact with foreign Jewish organizations ever resulted in acts of repression by the state. He replied, "In every town where Jewish life exists there are so-called *Landsmanshaften* clubs which keep up ties with similar clubs in foreign countries. What's more, the whole Jewish religious and cultural life is supported legally, materially, and morally by the government." He also told me that the Jews living in Poland today may emigrate to any country of their choice; some, however, have decided to remain and help build their socialist country.

Before we left Warsaw, we went one morning to the Church of the Saviour, located on the square of the same name. The church is one of 52 churches in the capital and one of nearly 900 in the country. It was restored to its prewar splendor through the financing of the state treasury. On the day we visited, about 400 people were at the early services, roughly half of whom were aged and an additional third were children. The remaining 10 percent consisted of teenagers and the middle-aged. I noticed the same proportion in other churches throughout the country. Most of the churchgoers seemed to be grandparents who had their small grandchildren in hand. The government does not interfere with the people's worship. In fact, the number of Roman Catholic churches and chapels has more than doubled since the Communists took power in Poland. What the Church no longer controls is the educational system. Prior to the Second World War, Roman Catholic teaching was compulsory in all primary and secondary schools. This is no longer the case. Now priests receive state salaries, and they cannot force religion on anyone. Religious training is confined to parish centers and is not extended to the schools. Poland's division between church and state is similar to that found in the United States.

One reason why the Roman Catholic Church has lost influence among the Polish people is that until only recently the Vatican refused to nominate permanent bishops to the western part of the country. This refusal was interpreted to mean that the Vatican believed that the settlement involving the western territories was only temporary and that the Germans might once again seize control of the region. Since Polish youth was made fully aware of the Church's attitude in the state-run schools, a special feeling of hostility toward the Vatican arose. However, when I talked to young people about Christianity, they continually stressed the idea that Christ was the first socialist and that through the ages He was bound by the priests first to feudalism and then to capitalism.

After services, we went fishing in the clean waters of the Vistula River with my brother Marion's family. The day was sunny and clear, and the water was quiet; nonetheless, no fish. When I asked my four-year-old nephew why, he replied seriously: "They probably went to church with my grandmother. And because Grandma walks so slow, they haven't come back to the water yet."

Chapter 10

Colors are still bashful;
therefore the quiet world, not to frighten them.
A bird-made dawn whistles joy and the first trains,
the song of the steam engines and the tune of the scythes.
A bluing sky darkens on high,
blind and newly born.

Thus the morning weather beautifully
approaches, humming, even to the windows,
grows the chirping, the azure drives itself around,
preparing to shoot out the sun against the window pane.
The boat of daybreak floats on our side.
Unpeopled yet, a sparrow's dawn.

———Jerzy Ficowski

Our next stop after Warsaw was Cracow. Our tickets were for two nonadjacent Pullman rooms and cost us 1,150 *zlotys* and 80 *grosze*, or roughly $34 on the official 1975 rate of exchange—inexpensive indeed by American standards. Between our two rooms we discovered an enormous man dressed in a bright blue jacket, yellow trousers, and red shoes, nervously smoking cigarette after cigarette. He claimed that he was buying dollars and gold watches.

The train left the station on time, at 11:50 P.M. Unlike our other experiences during our trip, we found this railroad to be as punctual and dependable as its personnel was efficient. While standing in the corridor, I noticed that it was difficult to distinguish travelers in Western Europe from those in Poland. An exception, perhaps, was the fat man we had seen earlier. We never discovered what he actually did, because we had to retire early to be refreshed for our 5:00 A.M. arrival in Cracow.

151

Cracow was the capital of Poland until the end of the sixteenth century. It was one of the few cities left untouched by the Second World War because, from the very outset of the conflict, it served as the center of the Germans' military operations in Poland. At the end of the war, the Germans completely mined the city, but the Soviet and Polish armies approached so fast that the Germans did not have time to detonate the mines. Thus, this urban architectural masterpiece was saved from destruction. In my mind, only Prague and Rome rival Cracow's beauty. The architectural crown of this city of 500,000 is Wawel Castle, an exquisite blend of Renaissance and Gothic architecture. Its most charming aspect is the central courtyard surrounded by delicately conceived porticos, galleries, balconies, and colonnades. Beneath the castle's fourteenth-century cathedral floor are the graves of Polish kings and national heroes.

As the train slowed down, we knew we were finally approaching this sleepy city. At the station we were greeted by the painter Jonasz Stern and his friend, the novelist, Kornel Filipowicz. Cracow seemed to be a very busy city this morning with people rushing to and from the station. In the air we smelled the fresh scent of flowers and blossoming maple trees. Everywhere we looked we saw very old buildings which gave us the impression that we had stepped back into the Middle Ages. The taxi driver who took us to the French Hotel, taking a cue from the lovely morning, was in a gay mood. Gloria and Anthony, eager to explore the city, pointed out the many structural delights that caught their eyes.

We left our bags in the lobby of the hotel and went to breakfast, which consisted of boiled eggs, ham, black bread, Chinese tea, and fresh milk. As we were leaving, we encountered the hotel's director on the lobby steps. I will forever remember his strong smell of alcohol, which was an insult to the beautiful morning. He whispered a polite excuse and then disappeared into his office. Despite this incident we had a pleasant stay at this hotel.

The majority of Polish hotels are controlled by the Orbis

Travel Agency, which during the sixties was directed by one of its operational wizards. One day I went to the director's office, full of complaints about service, but to my surprise left as peaceful as a spring lamb. The Poles now understand that, besides scenic attractions and good food, profitable tourism also demands fine hotels and service. Hotels have been steadily improving since my first visit in 1963.

Our first stop in Cracow was the cloth hall, Sukiennice, which was constructed in the fourteenth century in the center of the thousand-year-old marketplace. Fire razed it in the sixteenth century, and it was rebuilt during the next 200 years. This is the earliest and most beautiful example of the Polish Renaissance. In front of Sukiennice stands a monument to Poland's national poet, Adam Mickiewicz, and behind the building is the Gothic tower of the City Hall. Under the sturdy arcades of Sukiennice we bought some ice cream for ourselves and some crackers for the omnipresent pigeons.

We next saw the fortress Barbakan which was built in the fifteenth century as part of the defensive walls surrounding the city. The walls themselves are over ten feet thick, completely enveloping the old city with forty-seven Barbakan-shaped towers and eight gates and drawbridges. To this were added seven small observation towers with a so-called Florian Gate and 130 embrasures and crenels for an assortment of guns and instruments of warfare. Today, Barbakan serves as a stage for theatrical spectacles, including folk ballet and folk dancing. Trees shade three sides of the fortress; the fourth is open, creating a quaint atmosphere of bygone days.

Some years ago my children read about the trumpeter of Cracow who alerted the people from the higher tower of Saint Mary's Church that the Tartar army was approaching. Thus, we were all very interested in seeing the church and its two towers. The higher one is crested in Gothic style; from this tower a trumpeter announces every hour of the day. The second tower is of the Renaissance period, dating back to the sixteenth century; it is equipped with melancholy-sounding church bells. Inside, the church is cluttered with beautifully carved statues set against richly carved wooden paneling, and all through these chapels and in the nave are pockets of flowers. Above the altar is the sculpture masterpiece by Wit Stwosz, an exquisite maplewood polyptych that was taken by the Germans during the Second World War. It was recovered and has since been restored by Polish artists. The restoration of this fifteenth-century work required twenty years of continuous labor by one man, who carved individual likenesses of townspeople into the faces of the characters in those scenes surrounding the centerpiece of the altar.

Cracow served as one of the earliest European centers of knowledge. Its main science institute, the Cracow Academy, was built during the fourteenth century. While the Pope was engaged in the persecution of Galileo, the academy attracted Europe's best scientific scholars, including Filippo Buonaccorsi Callimachus and Copernicus. The oldest part of this university, the Collegium Maius, was constructed in 1364 during the reign of King Casimir Jagiello, and it houses fantastic treasures and antiques.

When we left this part of Cracow, Anthony suggested that we see Nowa Huta.

"I know what you'd like to do," replied his mother. "You'd like to compare the old with the new."

"Doesn't everybody?" asked Gloria.

Until 1950, Nowa Huta was an ordinary suburban village called Mogila, meaning "grave." Today, this "village" is inhabited by over 100,000 people and has many modern apartment buildings and beautiful parks and gardens. Most of the workers in this unusual town are employed in the local metallurgical combine where they produce one-third of the national output of iron, steel, and other metal products. The apartments have three or four rooms and are equipped with washing machines, refrigerators, television sets, and radios. The children ride their bicycles in newly constructed playgrounds. On weekends, families who own their automobiles drive to the nearby lakes to fish or to sightsee.

After we saw Nowa Huta, we visited the painter Stern and the writer Filipowicz. I have never seen such fishing enthusiasts as these two. In Filipowicz's home the bathtub was full of live fish and green mossy slime which Anthony vividly remembers to this day. Their conversations consisted of fishing expeditions, politics, and art, in that order. They always argued these subjects very bitterly, but I never saw such a friendship as that which existed between this short, haggard, sour-expressioned artist and tall, thin aristocratic-looking writer. Both of them had been in German concentration camps and both had managed to escape, but with their health permanently affected. It was only by a miracle that Stern escaped execution: because of the large number of victims assembled for the mass murder, he was only wounded and re-mained beneath a pile of corpses until nighttime when he fled. Filipowicz wrote a book about his friend's experience.

Stern and I walked many hours on Cracow's streets. During our walk, many people greeted him with reverence as well as friendliness. He was then chancellor of the 400-student Academy of Arts in Cracow, which, along with the one in Warsaw, is the most prestigious in Poland. The building which houses the academy is a spacious, solidly built structure that resembles a museum. It contains numerous originals or copies of Greek and Roman sculpture, as well as paintings and weapons used by the Poles when they were a warlike kingdom 500 years ago. Stern's office was a large, high-ceilinged room. On the walls were dis-played portraits, mostly self-portraits, of the past chancellors who were elected to a three-year term by the faculty.

After sightseeing, we saw Shakespeare's *The Merry Wives of Windsor* at the invitation of Marion Kramarski, director of the Slowacki Theater. Before the performance, the literary director of the theater, Alfred Woycik, kindly told us stories about one of its great actors, Ludwik Solski, who lived to be a hundred and acted until his death. One day, he told us, a young actor approached Solski with a complaint that women made him so panicky that he could not even conceive of marriage. "That is the very reason why you should marry," the old actor replied. "Because right now you are afraid of all women, and when you get married you'll be afraid of only one."

Chapter 11

at the storm's end
            when fragrant earth gripped
urgent as a prayer
            and silence after thunder shouted the heart's thought
                        there is a sudden paradise of colored air
                                                by beauty fevered
            by beauty overwrought

            o
            blame me not
            deliriums honest rest
            that took her
            to my breast

We left Cracow by bus for Zakopane on a warm, sunny day. As soon as we left the city, we were moving through blankets of green and gold, clinging to the narrow road that led to the Tatra Mountains, the most picturesque part of the Carpathian chain. Our neighbor on the bus was Gustaw Holoubek, the highly original Shakespearean actor with whom we had a lively discussion on the American theater. He had never been to the United States, but his knowledge of Broadway and off-Broadway productions was that of a native. We suspected that he had a regular subscription to *Variety*. It started raining, and a terrific mountain wind lashed the trees groundward, but our bus continued climbing.

When we reached Zakopane, it was still raining, and Holoubek suggested we stay in his hotel which was reserved exclusively for actors. The hotel had no room for us, however. We could not find a taxi, but luckily we were offered a ride in a private car supplied by one of Holoubek's friends. We were soon at the Imperial Hotel. Standing on the steps was a charming receptionist by the name of Helena Szluinska, a striking woman with ebony hair, black shining eyes, and bright white teeth. She gave us two rooms which, with three meals, cost us 408 *zlotys* per day—or twelve dollars—an extremely reasonable price for large quarters with balconies and for a long list of meats and fish. To encourage us to take excursions into the mountains, the hotel offered, at no charge, sandwiches, milk or tea, and fruits.

The Tatra Mountains made a tremendous impression on my family; they still talk about the peaks which bordered Morskie Oko Lake and the phantasmagoric display of clouds above them. They remember, too, their excursion to the Koscieliska Valley, their walk in the fragrant beech, pine, spruce, and cedar groves, and the awesome view of this whole chain of rugged mountains from the peak of Gubalowka.

Zakopane is the winter capital of Poland. Polish skiing was born here. The Polish 1972 gold medal winner in ski jumping, Fortuna, was also born here. In this town, world ski competitions were held in 1929, 1939, and 1962.

Because of its geographical position, Zakopane is the most important center for all Polish winter sports. From here one can see daily expeditions departing for the mountains as well as numerous foreign visitors admiring the splendor of the Tatra. Gentle hills surrender to two sides of Zakopane and present exciting opportunities for beginning skiers. In addition to modern equipment, a well-trained staff of instructors is available to novice skiers. For the more advanced, cable cars run from Zakopane to Kasprowy Wierch and Gubalowka. From there, skiers can enjoy the space which is ideal for their sport. At different points throughout the mountains are small, cosy rest cottages, manned by professional rescuers who are on alert twenty-four hours a day in the winter.

Anthony was especially taken by the breathtaking surroundings, and I could see him furiously scribbling away in his diary. Later, intrigued by the energy he displayed upon coming to Zakopane, I asked him for a sample of what he had written.

For the first time since June twelfth, my sneezing stopped; to breathe is like eating mint. Today we took a cable car up to the top of the mountains. The ride was in two parts, the second part being more interesting. We passed over a large area of pine trees which thinned out into bare rock and a sort of hardy green shrub which covered sections of the rock in clumps. At the end of the ride was a large building which housed a restaurant and a souvenir shop. Outside, the air was cold and occasionally an icy wind would crack at our hands and faces. When the wind wasn't blowing, there was complete silence, as if in a void. For miles down into the valley and up into the mist-shrouded peaks nothing could be heard. The effect was numbing. Everywhere there was silence, and then a wind would hit your frozen hands and red face. I walked a ways up a small wall of rock to reach one of the peaks, and running down this chain of rock like a backbone was the border between Czechoslovakia and Poland. When I reached the top, I saw mist blowing all about me and, every so often, a rip in it would reveal the full expanse of the valley below. Down over 2,000 feet I could see ants—people walking around the glacial lakes. On the Czech side a green valley stretched from 200 feet below me all the way to the bottom of the valley and up to the other side, a distance I could not judge accurately. On my left was a snow-covered peak, glistening in the sunlight that had dropped through the moving fog.

That afternoon the key clerk at the hotel, Jan Gasienica, took us in his Russian-built auto through a vast pine forest, after which we visited the house where Lenin lived during his 1914 conspiracy. We then visited a curve in the road where I saw the most beautiful mountain I have ever seen. It was in Czechoslovakia.

Today was less cold than yesterday and the fog was somewhat thinned. I bought a chess set for 900 *zlotys*. In the afternoon we visited Morskie Oko, the largest natural glacial lake in Poland. The terrain was rugged and consistent in its beauty. An immense forest of fir trees blanketed the lower slopes and above them rose the barren rock, which in some cases was shrouded.

When you get older you begin to cherish peace, and perhaps the most important peace to attain is family peace. And so it is that I also submit my daughter's description.

The fog clothed the mountains with soft swirling whiteness. Only to be pushed away by winds. It was today that I was going in the cable car to Kasprowy Wierch mountain. It was bitter cold but the view was wonderful. Fir trees covered the mountains while three big lakes shone through them. My poor ears. . . . After lunch I went on a ride again. I am happy here. The forest is lovely.

In the morning we went shopping. The stores are very colorful and I liked the souvenir shops best. I bought an elephant pin made out of ivory and for my brother a beautiful chess set hand-carved out of wood with colorful mountaineer figures.

Later, we went to Morskie Oko. The road was very winding, and the man who was driving us said it was used before the war for car-racing tournaments. The pine trees which bordered the road looked dense as though someone had planted them purposely to keep people out. Moss was strewn around; it looked like a blanket. Morskie Oko is the largest glacial lake in Poland. It was beautiful! Rocks bordered it ready to create a landslide. I and my brother sweatingly climbed the mountain. Mom and Dad only went halfway. The mountains were covered with rocks and snow and sparse vegetation. We had trouble trying to open the canteens and we were very thirsty.

Later we walked past the rusty cans of tar, looking at the houses and scenery. We looked inside the mountain church. It was homely and everything was wood and made by the people themselves. Outside was an enclosed portion of land with flowers and a statue of Saint Mary. Next we stopped at Lenin's Museum, which used to be his house. A young girl showed us things which he used when he lived there.

When we were tired we went home to shower. The steam from the hot water rose in clouds of misty hotness. After lunch we went by car to the top of the mountains and stopped when we reached a dead end. We had to walk the rest of the way. The scenery was breathtaking, tall walls of stone bordered the rocky path. Flowers grew along the sides of our way. A stream rushed by, tearing up rocks and dirt. We reached the rest area, where a small house was standing, before the rain came down. After soda and candy we continued climbing.

My family was so captivated by the Tatra Mountains that they decided to stay another week. And I, already knowing the Polish mountains, went by myself to the western part of Poland which had experienced a postwar renaissance. During the war, almost every German farmer or factory owner had employed slave labor. As the war was ending, they feared reprisals from the approaching Soviet and Polish armies, and so, when the German army retreated, much of the German population went with them. The Polish population that was left undertook the rebuilding of the area's churches, farms, factories, towns, and cities. They were helped by the six million other Poles who shifted west when the eastern territory was incorporated into the Soviet Union. While the birth rate increased from three to ten births per thousand in the central part of Poland, the figure was almost twenty per thousand in the western section.

At seven o'clock in the morning I took a bus from Zakopane to Katowice, the "Polish Pittsburgh." The countryside was hilly and flooded with morning sunlight. At the crossing of the road was an amusing sign: "Drive slow and you will see a beautiful lake; drive fast and you will see the police." On the hills lay many huts covered with shingles and surrounded by orchards, stacks of hay, sheep, and cows. On the roads some people were dressed in mountaineers' suits, while others traveled in their ready-made factory outfits. Children were riding on bicycles, on horses, and in buses—lots of children, because this was vacation time.

It took me half an hour to reach the town of Nowy Targ. The

OCHNIO

a scene from "Replika," a play using no words, only images, based on the concentration camp experience of the author Jozef Szajna, who is an innovative theatrical director

a scene from Tomaszewski's famous Polish Pantomime Theater

CAF

Lidia Zamkow is a leading director of Polish Theater and television.

American playwright Arthur Miller obviously approves the production of his "Incident in Vichy" in conversation with former director of the Polish Theater Jerzy Jasienski and critic Roman Szydlowski.

Lerner & Loewe's "My Fair Lady" was popular at the Comedy Theater in Warsaw.

TOPIENSKI

Mazowsze is the national folk dance company.

Carpathian mountaineers are also famed for their colorful dances.

Mine workers near Cracow carved this altar sculpture out of salt. It appears in an entirely underground church in Wieliczka.

wayside shrine near Cracow

detail of the Wit Stwosz Altar

fifteenth century Wit Stwosz Altar in St. Mary's Church, Cracow

MOREK

CAF

He couldn't wait to get home.

CAF

village children learning to sculpt

Warsaw's International Book Fair draws large crowds.

Polish shoppers browse in a supermarket in Warsaw.

MOREK

Cracow, like many cities, is full of pigeons.

CAF

Warsaw has lovely sidewalk cafes.

Beaches on the Baltic are very popular.

the author (center) and his family, shooting the rapids on the Dunajec River—a unique tourist attraction

first thing I saw there was a brass orchestra on horseback playing Polish marches and leading a wedding procession into a church. Behind them came a colorfully painted carriage drawn by two gray stallions; inside sat the young couple, dressed in their Sunday mountaineer's suits. A dozen mounted young men completed the procession. Today, most weddings are conducted by civilian officials and a church wedding is no longer required by law. In Warsaw, for example, it is a familiar sight to see men clad in black formal suits and top hats and ladies in brightly colored flowered hats and gowns, all posing in front of the building where civil marriages are performed. On another occasion you might see a bicycle brigade with riders clad for a race en route to this same building.

One time in Warsaw I saw a procession led by a motorized rickshaw in which the couple was dressed in white nuptial finery. They were escorted by men on roller skates. I followed them inside. The room was full of flowers and the appropriate music. The official had already begun the ceremony when I heard a commotion in the back and a woman's voice yelled out, "Finally I found you!" She rushed up to the front, grabbed the groom by the hand, and pulled him outside. The official shrugged his shoulders. "Perhaps it's his mother, or perhaps his first love."

In front of me on the bus to Katowice sat a peasant woman with two small boys. One boy was reading an illustrated magazine while the other was restless and making quite a bit of noise. The one reading the book exclaimed, "Mother, mother, don't you see the poor fish on the hook?" As he jerked the magazine before his mother's eyes, I too had a chance to look at it. I recognized the fisherman in the picture as the artist Jonasz Stern, but I had no chance to comment because the other boy said, "Poor fish, poor fish." The mother turned her sunburned face to her son and said, "Why is she so poor? If she hadn't opened her mouth she wouldn't have gotten a hook in it. So you better watch your mouth."

In my travels it was heartening to see the large numbers of peasants on buses and trains, in the theater, as I have noted earlier, and even at painting exhibitions and art shows. Education is now part of their lives, because with modern communication and transportation systems they are no longer confined to their villages.

During my four-hour trip from Zakopane to Upper Silesia, on both sides of the road I noticed many new brick buildings which were completed or nearly so; most of them were single-family houses. Upper Silesia is a network of small towns clustered around coal and iron mines and all kinds of factories and industrial establishments. Everywhere you see chimneys with black, blue, red, and yellow smoke billowing out. The center of this part of the country is Katowice with 300,000 people. The real wealth of this region is coal, which the geologists have estimated consists of some 300 billion tons; to this date the miners have brought up only 3 billion tons as they work through the 110 mines.

Katowice is extremely active, heavily trafficked, and clouded with soot and smog most of the time. Yet, I have never seen so many people dressed in white, especially women and young girls, almost in defiance of the ever-present dirt and factory dust. The people of this region love sports, especially hockey and soccer. Silesia has more fields that are used solely for sports activities than any other section of Poland.

At the bus stop my journalist friend Jacek, his wife Ewa, and their seven-year-old son Wojtek were waiting for me. Jacek was six feet tall, blond with blue eyes, and the grandson of a famous head of Cracow University. His businesslike approach to my trip would have amazed even an American. Immediately, he took me to the Café Silesia for a bite to eat and for a discussion of a tour of the city. On the way there, he asked me about Warsaw and his three favorite Polish novelists: Jerzy Andrzejewski, Kazimierz Brandys, and Stanislaw Grochowiak. He was curious to know my opinion about their latest books. His question prompted me to ask whether he was writing himself and was thus considering them as competitors. He replied with a smile, "Yes." The next thing I asked him about was the contents of his new novel.

"My novel is based on a real happening," he began.

"It must be a very dramatic incident in your life if you are writing about it."

He began telling me the story. "One day when I was working for the *Western Daily*, a young man walked into the office and said that his adopted mother, a German, told him that his name was Bogumil Uniowski. The Nazis had taken him from his Polish mother and presented him to a German family, who removed him to Bonn before the advancing eastern front could reach Katowice. Today the young Bogumil, who didn't speak a word of Polish, had returned to his native town to look for his Polish mother.

"A few weeks after I wrote about this boy in the newspaper, a middle-aged woman dressed in a Silesian costume with faded ribbons and an old amber necklace, probably her best clothing, I thought, came into my office. She was the boy's real mother. Later I discovered that she was wearing this very outfit the day her son was taken away from her. I brought mother and son together, who both burst out crying, he speaking German and she Polish. They left arm in arm and I was happy for them."

"Is this the end of the story?" asked Jacek's small son, who had a sad expression on his face.

The father looked at Wojtek and then at me and continued. "Not quite. After a few months the same woman appeared in my office dressed in rags and weeping. 'My son beats me all the time and calls me all kinds of German names and throws me out of my own house to which he has been bringing all sorts of young German friends who drink and break everything as well as play with guns.' I decided to investigate and after a while discovered that her son was educated in the true Nazi spirit, with hate and contempt for other nationalities and for old people. Although he had moments of understanding and compassion, he spent most of the time drinking and beating his mother. The old woman didn't want to go to the police because she didn't want to ruin her son's reputation. So she returned to me to complain. In this part of the country we have many such cases which are stranger than fiction and as difficult to solve." After a short pause, he concluded philosophically, "Why don't we have the same witnesses to our defeat as to our victory?"

"Because there are many things which surround us over which we have no control," I tried to explain, "and the same events heal wounds in some hearts while making fresh wounds in other ones."

Katowice City, which had more than doubled its population from the prewar figure, had two main problems. One was the constant need for experienced workers in mines and factories which were being steadily modernized. The other difficulty was getting proper structural support for the buildings that rested on or near areas hollowed out in tapping the coal deposits. The city was continuously receiving engineering assistance from all over the country. But today's engineers rely more and more on mechanical devices, and these are limited, as my friend explained. To illustrate his point, Jacek told me of his brother, who one day came home from work very tired. When his wife asked him what had happened, he replied simply, "We were working on some crucially important problem, and in the midst of solving it the computers went to pieces and we were forced to think."

Despite all its problems, Katowice is a most prosperous town, as you can judge by the well-dressed people, the fully stocked store windows, and the crowded restaurants. In the restaurant we went to, we waited almost half an hour for a table, and when we got it two men approached us and asked if the they might occupy the two extra chairs. One of them was a dramatist, Andrzej Wydrynski, whose play *Sun Going Around the Earth* was playing in the widely separated cities of Berlin, Rio de Janeiro, and Tel Aviv. The other fellow was Wilhelm Szewczyk, a novelist and essayist, who weighed over 300 pounds and appropriately ate and talked a lot. For lunch he had three small lobsters, filet mignon, and a bottle of Caucasian cognac, in true epicurean style.

After our introduction, Szewczyk related this anecdote: "During the Soviet army's return from Berlin, I was in the town of Zawiercie. While walking past a market where they were hanging a portrait of Stalin, I noticed an old woman staring very hard at it. She glanced at me and asked, 'Who is this gentleman whom they are hanging?'

"'The Marshal,' I said to her with dignity.'

"'Marshal Pilsudski?'

"'Oh, no.'

"'Then who is he?'

"'Stalin; Pilsudski died a long time ago.'

"'And what did this Marshal Stalin do for Poland?'

"'He chased Hitler from Poland.'

"'Oh, mister, mister—and who will chase Marshal Stalin from Silesia?'"

To see how life was progressing in Zawiercie, I took a drive there with Jacek. At first glance you see only old one-story houses. But when you look more closely, you see blocks and blocks of new apartments, separately and in clusters. While the buildings are uniformly of concrete and brick, lots of flowers planted in front of them give them a more cheerful aspect. Through the city flows the Warta River. The river's waters are clean, even though multitudes of chimneys project into the sky. We learned later that all factories are required to deposit their refuse, whether solid or liquid, in special bins so as not to pollute the rivers and lakes.

Throughout Zawiercie we noticed that trees had been newly planted and that new street lights had been installed to add more life and color; the town squares were choked with trees and flowers in bloom. Throughout the day one sees people traveling to and from the factories, many of whom carry briefcases or lunch boxes. This town is almost completely populated by workers. To see how they lived, I visited one of the houses standing on the edge of a group of new apartment buildings. I knocked on the door, and it was opened by a man in his fifties. His name was Franciszek Stary and he worked in a cotton factory. His wife, a woman of about his age, was busy preparing a meal. They were pleasant and willing to answer my questions. I discovered that they lived with their daughter and her two children in two rooms and a kitchen. I looked around the rooms and noticed old furniture that was well kept and polished. In the kitchen an old refrigerator was standing and in one of the other rooms, a new television set. I asked the man if it wasn't difficult to support his family and grandchildren on his factory earnings alone. He replied, "We do have two salaries between my daughter and myself. It's not that bad, but the only thing is that this house is old and we've been waiting two years for an apartment in a new building."

From the Starys I learned that the demand for new housing remained high in Zawiercie. The housing shortage stemmed from the prewar government's low priority on new housing and from the fact that during the war over 20 percent of all housing units in the country were destroyed beyond repair. As a result, over two-thirds of all capital invested in housing since the Second World War has come from the government.

To see what people can buy in appliance stores, I went to one of the largest in town and discovered that the greatest demand was for refrigerators, bicycles, and kitchenware. I asked the store manager what the town worker's approximate minimum salary was. He said about 3,000 *zlotys* per month for a factory worker and 2,700 *zlotys* for a worker in an auto repair shop.

My next stop was an employment office, where a dozen or so people were in the waiting room. Every few minutes a man would come out of the office and announce various openings in local factories. Invariably, the same questions were shouted. "How much does it pay?"

"Is it heavy work?" The women were the most particular about types of employment; they did not want to work in a cotton factory or any place where they would have to produce a minimum amount daily. They were primarily interested in light work in modern stores and offices, but most of them lacked the necessary qualifications for such positions. I asked the head of the employment office if the applicants were always so demanding. His reply was the standard one I heard throughout the country: "There is plenty of work, so much so that people can afford to choose what they want to do. Sometimes they wait months. Today over 22,000 people work in large factories and in 150 smaller establishments in our city. And every day there are a few hundred openings for office and factory workers. Despite the extensive training programs all over the country, it is difficult to find qualified persons. Since we are a socialist country, there are no bread lines or unemployment lines and no crime bred by such conditions. It is possible to have no inflation and no unemployment. To do this, you must have a state-run economy and no class of wealthy individuals who waste resources in luxury consumption.''

After I left the unemployment office, I paid a visit to a spot a few hundred yards behind the city hall. There stood a miniature pine forest and behind it new apartment houses for approximately 1,000 families. Most of them were young people with two or three small children. For them the city fathers had built three new schools which cost approximately 30 million *zlotys*. These school buildings had huge windows, no bars or barbed wire, and no security guards. I went to the main building and asked to see the principal whereupon a woman in her forties appeared. When I asked her what kind of problems she faced with her charges, she replied that the children of today were less spoiled and more eager to learn than prewar children. Practically everyone, she said, wanted to be an engineer. I asked her what was behind the widespread interest in this field.

"Maybe because the parents are always talking about cars—how to buy them, how to fix them," she explained, smiling. "Do you know what the biggest problem is in our town? It's garages. Everyone wants to have a garage. The people in Zawiercie are crazy about cars, motorcycles, and motorbikes."

Not all the people in the town lived in apartment houses. One person I met, a fifty-eight-year-old named Jan Dudzik, was a minor official in the city hall. He had purchased a piece of land on the other side of a pine forest and had built himself a two-family brick house.

"How did you learn how to build?" I asked him.

"Before the war I was a carpenter, and during the war, I learned something about masonry. As a man coming from a peasant family I have always desired to own my own house."

"Where did you get enough money to build such a house?" I inquired.

"As an official, it is true, I don't make much money, but I do manage to save—and very carefully. I also spent two years working in the Polish Embassy in Washington, so I saved then too."

The house looked professionally built; it was almost completed on the outside and had a shingled roof. Inside there were no bathtubs, nor any interior design as yet, but Mr. Dudzik said that next year he would move his family in.

On my trip around the city I estimated that there were about 800 private single-family houses, and, according to my information, all of them were built as private enterprises.

On my return to the hotel I went into the restaurant for a cup of coffee. When I had tasted it, I asked the waiter, "Is this coffee or soup?"

He replied, "Anything you wish it to be. If you think it's soup, it will, of course, cost more. But if you insist it's coffee, then it will be less."

Afterward, I went up to my room, where two friends were waiting for me. The first one was Tamekczyz, an engineer with broad shoulders and workers' hands. When the war ended, he was only a mechanic's helper, but through the Workers' Organization he had been sent to technical schools, and in four years, after studying and working and stealing time from his wife and children, he finally had gotten his diploma as an engineer. Although he had a good factory job, it did not satisfy him. He felt he did not have enough knowledge for the position and that people could not trust his technical know-how. To get additional training was difficult, however, for he had a family to support. Finally, he had decided to go to night school for another four years, had received a master's degree in engineering. He was now the director of a factory but was still looking forward to getting his doctorate.

The other friend awaiting me was also a self-made man. Originally a welder, he was now an engineer and head of the local National Council in his town. His best friend, Bernard Bugdol, was once a coal miner who was producing four times above the normal quota. Later, Bugdol had decided to study. With the help of local officials, he became an engineer in four years; finally he headed the Lagiewniki coal mine.

A second group of career people in Poland is made up of the younger generation who received their education after the war without any sacrifices or worries about tuition or their next meal. During the twelve years between 1951 and 1963, the Silesian Polytechnic awarded 4,000 diplomas to members of this group, 70 percent of whom come from workers' families.

A third group is the largest, the youngest, and the one that grew up under the most normal conditions. They come to Silesia from various polytechnic schools all over the country, equipped with an excellent basic education which is achieved independently of family sacrifices and night courses. All their training is owed to state support. They work in Silesia's mines and factories, rebuilding and modernizing them. This group is made up of 15,000 engineers and represents the purest efforts thus far of this socialist society. They have made the greatest contributions to the technical and social progress now taking place in Silesia.

Chapter 12

the wind is in the trees
like flickering flame
sweeping an autumntuned
and golddrenched
lyre
> *garden*
> *what is your name*
> *what colored symphonies*
> *spread wings of fire*
> *for lovers flight*
> *through changing landscape*
> *nevermore the same*
in a rustling shimmer
we whisper ardently
> *the leaves hold the light*
> *of your face*
in bright battalions
whose banners hang
> *from every sparkling bough*
> *to hail heart's victory*
this is a purple dream
the trees are sending
no words
> *can shape its telling   oh how*
> *could we foresee or how declare*
> *this miracle*
> > *of spring*
> > *with*
> > *autumn blending*

184

The most unusual attraction of Silesia is Chelmska Mountain, also known as Saint Anna, which lies on the flat terrain of the Opole district. On the side of this mountain is a monument celebrating the Silesian insurrectionists who fought against the Germans. The famous Polish sculptor Xawery Dunikowski fashioned this stark landmark. From the top of the mountain all one sees for miles around is flat land with its fields and forests intersected by newly constructed white roads. Also visible in the distant horizons are church towers and factory chimneys which are partially obscured by clouds of cement dust against the blue sky.

Chelmska Mountain, over 1,400 feet high, is composed of limestone deposits on a hard base of basalt. Archeological discoveries made on this mountain prove that Slavic tribes inhabited the area before the Iron and Bronze Ages and that they worshipped pagan gods. Christianity filtered into Poland over 1,000 years ago, and a chapel was built here during the sixteenth century. Later, the Saint Anna Church was built on this site, thus giving the mountain its modern name. Melchior Gasyn, a Polish magnate from the town of Wielun, erected a Franciscan monastery on the mountain, but when Poland lost her independence to her three neighbors during the eighteenth century, the Prussian rulers took over the church and monastery and banished the Polish inhabitants. They nevertheless failed to halt the pilgrimage of Silesians to the top of the mountain, where they would pray for their country's independence. In May, 1921, Silesians took up arms against the foreign occupiers and fought a brave battle at the foot of this mountain. The Silesians were defeated and did not regain their territory until January, 1945, when the Polish army liberated the mountain and all of the Silesia.

I used to know Xawery Dunikowski, who lived until the ripe old age of ninety. I'll never forget the first time I spoke to him. He told me that during his youth in Paris he was thin and undernourished. One day a wealthy American doctor visited him in his studio and told him, "I don't think I care to order any more of your sculpture, as you don't look to me as if you're going to live very long."

"How long do you think I am going to live?" Dunikowski asked the doctor.

"Come down tomorrow to my hospital and I will examine you."

After a sleepless night, the sculptor visited the hospital, and after the examination steeled himself for the inevitable question, "So what do you think, will I die soon?"

"Yes," the doctor admitted. A deep concern showed on his face, because he had made an advance payment on some sculptures that Dunikowski had not yet completed.

Dunikowski then turned smilingly to me, "You know, he was right to worry—one year after he examined me he died."

To be in Silesia and not visit the Slask Group, known for their songs and dancing, is perhaps analogous to being in Rome and not visiting the Vatican. This famous ensemble lives in a fourteenth-century castle of 200 rooms in the town of Koszecin. Ten years after the end of the Second World War, the musicologist and specialist in Silesian folklore Stanislaw Hadyna and the choreographer Elwira Kaminska organized a regional group of folk dancers. Eventually, this group grew to 300 people and is presently known worldwide through its performances in over 100 countries. Only those who have completed formal ballet training can apply, and then the applicants are very carefully screened from all over Poland. The competition is quite stiff; Hadyna and Kaminska interview several thousand boys and girls, and among them they find only a few new talents each year. Each day rehearsals begin at 9:00 A.M. and continue until 2:00 P.M. When the troupe is preparing to go on tour, however, they frequently work all night. Hadyna demands perfection, regardless of whether they appear in a large city or a small rural town. They may remain in the group as dancers for only six to ten years, after which they must leave either to become dance teachers or to perform on their own. Under the aegis of the Ministry of Cultural Affairs, the directors provide these young artists with the necessary background in music and higher education, in addition to superb dance training, so that they can continue growing as artists.

When I visited the Slask Group, they had just returned from a tour of Europe and Asia, from Paris to Mongolia. They allowed me to see their collection of 1,000 costumes based on details found in legends and stories.

Before I left this part of the country, my host, Jacek, took me in his car to the town of Ruda Slaska to see the old soldier Jozef Garbas. The story of his leadership in Silesia's fight for independence after the First World War revolves around a company flag. The flag was not made of silk, brocade, or any expensive cloth; it was simply a red flag made from a pillowcase. On one side was crudely embroidered a Polish eagle, and on the other was the face of the Holy Mother. Showing it to me, Garbas said, "Today, as you can see, there is not much left of the eagle, or of the Holy Mother, and even the color of the flag has faded. So many years. At that time we didn't have money for a flag. We had time only for fighting. The first hole in this flag was made by a boy named Jan Golawski, who carried it with his gun. When his gun went off accidentally, the bullet pierced it. Our company of 130 boys took up positions in Sucholonie with old-fashioned rifles against an enemy equipped with machine guns. But luckily we were hidden in a tall wheatfield. When they finally discovered our position, they opened fire. Jan was hit, and as he fell, mortally wounded, he passed the flag to the soldier closest to him, Jozef Sliwa. But just as Jozef reached for it, machinegun fire split his head; this also happened to the next soldier who tried to take the flag from Jozef. Under the Germans' fierce firepower, we decided to retreat and regroup. That evening as we calculated our losses, we discovered that our leader, Malcher Mrozek, had been killed. During the night we returned to look for him and we found his body lying among the tall weeds. We knew that our town remained in German hands. So we picked up our company flag and left for the neighboring town to wait for the time when we would return.

"When Germany attacked Poland in 1939, we didn't have a chance to fight, so we put our flag in a can and buried it in the garden of Wladyslaw Draganczyk. One day three S. S. men came to his house and beat him, shouting, '*Wo ist die verfluchte Blut-*

fahne?' He didn't answer, and so they took him to a concentration camp. In 1940, Draganczyk escaped and returned to his farm just long enough to dig up the flag. He gave it to his mother-in-law, who was the owner of a casket store. She kept the flag in the most expensive casket, knowing no one would be likely to buy it. While the flag was in its cozy hiding place, the members of our group were diminishing. Two of them died in concentration camps, four in the underground movement, and the rest came to be scattered all over the world. Draganczyk had been recaptured and sent to a different concentration camp. Eventually, he and I became the only survivors of the First World War skirmish. In January, 1945, we returned to our homes. The first place we went was the casket store, where we pulled the flag out and, like two crazy fellows, paraded through the town. People who saw us stopped and began to cry."

On my way to the city of Wroclaw, I stopped in the old town of Opole. I was eager to explore this town whose buildings gave off an aura of friendliness through its green, orange, and yellow walls. The most impressive sight was the ruins of an old castle; only the tower had been left standing by the enemy because it was not worth destroying. From this medieval castle, princes of the Piast dynasty ruled this part of the country; today they all lie in elaborate tombs under the church. When you walk through the marketplace which was constructed by the present socialist government, you feel that you have returned to the Renaissance.

The countryside surrounding Opole was covered with fields of ripe wheat and barley that day, and all around was the scent of flowers and honey. In the meadows old women tended geese, while black-and-white-dappled cows sauntered leisurely. Around the houses were vegetable gardens. On the roads people rode on bicycles and carts, bringing hay from the fields to the villages. From time to time, a truck loaded with coal passed the children playing on the edge of the roads.

The farmers of the Opole district are famous for their high agricultural output. The production of honey, a very recent de-

velopment, is another source of pride. Grodkow County leads in
the quantity produced, followed by Brzeg, Nisa, and Kluczbork
counties. Some beehives produce over eighty pounds of honey per
season. In the Opole district there is an organization of honey
farmers with more than 3,000 members who control about 60,000
beehives. Through special cross-breeding they have developed
their own bees which they call *opolanka*. Jan Dzierzon, the
"Copernicus" of beehives, was born in Kluczbork County. He
revolutionized the industry completely and discovered numerous
new facts about bees for which he was honored by many European
governments. Legends even circulated about him, one of which
maintains that he charmed the bees into producing more without
their stinging him. He was also reported to be seen naked in
the fields with a swarm of bees around him. His success made
him famous and wealthy. One day when he was gravely ill and a
doctor from town was summoned to his hut, one of the jealous
peasants asked the doctor whether there was any hope that he
would live.

"It depends on what you're hoping for," the doctor replied,
"his living or his dying."

Jan Dzierzon was a great man because of his communion with
nature, but his fellow farmers did not like him. It seems that a
native son can never make miracles in his own village.

I left Opole, and at 10:00 A.M. I arrived in Wroclaw where a
friend of my brother Marion was waiting for me at the railroad
station. Ignacy was a young man of about thirty-six, a journalist
with a pale face, long nose, and green eyes. He was over six feet
tall and wore an orange jacket, khaki trousers, and light-brown
shoes. As we walked out of the station, he pointed with pride to the
many flowers gracing the building.

Inhabited by half a million people living on the banks of the
Oder River, Wroclaw is the center of culture and industry in Lower
Silesia. The red, blue, and green city hall, which was begun in the
fourteenth century, has been restored to its Gothic beauty. On the
tower of the hall is a 400-year-old clock with four faces whose
punctuality is the mayor's pride. The Oder River, which slices

through the city with its many branches and tributaries, divides the city into twelve sections that are connected by numerous bridges. The old thirteenth-century cathedral, one of the most interesting buildings in the city, is another postwar architectural restoration. Wroclaw has eight university schools and 600 industrial establishments; Pafawag is the largest factory and produces railroad cars and electrical appliances. The name of the city is derived from the old Polish name *Wrocislaw*, which literally means a man returning to his native place or regaining his fame. The father of the city was Boleslaw Iwaszkiewicz, by education a mathematician and by profession the mayor. He was well over sixty years of age, but his short haircut and trim figure gave him the appearance of a much younger man. He and his wife (who is also a mathematician) lived in a three-room apartment; as they had no children, they did not need larger quarters. Iwaszkiewicz is an amateur photographer of long standing and has collected pictures illustrating the destruction and reconstruction of the city. His second hobby is music.

Mayor Iwaszkiewicz begins his day at 6:45 A.M. with a light breakfast and then he walks to his office. "The first time I walked to my office was in August, 1945, when the city was 70 percent in ruins with no canals, no telephones, no transportation. The 150,000 people who had survived the war and who had stayed here were either old or sick." He stressed the word "old" and then he stressed its opposite. "Today, half of the city's population is under eighteen years of age. These young people, together with the many new buildings, give Wroclaw a feeling of vitality and hope."

In the tenth century, Wroclaw was already a center for Catholic bishops. By the twelfth century, with King Boleslaw Wrymouth's victory over the Germans at Dogs' Field, the rapid development of Wroclaw began. The city established cultural and trade contacts with Poland proper and with France, Italy, Ireland, Russia, and Byzantium as well. In the middle of the eighteenth century, it was captured by the Germans who closed the university and dissolved the city's independent government. The high taxes

levied on the burghers ruined all cultural and economic development. Life improved for a short time during the nineteenth century
when Wroclaw reestablished economic contact with Poland. Then
more Polish was spoken on the streets and more Polish signs
appeared in the stores. In 1921, despite more than 100 years of
German persecution and extermination, an Association of Polish
People was established with 20,000 members. The final attempt at
exterminating the Polish people, of course, came with Adolf
Hitler.

The best view of the progress being made in reconstructing
this part of the country may be had by going to the periphery of the
city where new housing projects for the new population are multi-
plying. Year after year new buildings spring up in the center and
around the city's marketplace where a 217-foot tower dominates
the Gothic city hall.

At a distance from this site, on Solny Place, stand two
beautiful old houses; one is "Under the Griffin" and the other,
"Under the Gold Crown." Other Gothic edifices which have been
thoroughly restored are the Church of the Holy Cross and the
Church of Mary Magdalene. Wroclaw Cathedral, which was
begun during the middle of the twelfth century and completed 100
years later, was 80 percent destroyed during the Second World
War. It was rebuilt by the present government with the characteristic care given to historical monuments in Poland. The most interesting secular baroque architecture in Europe is Wroclaw University with its tremendous hall where every year young people
begin their academic careers with a colorful ceremony. But youth
takes the older generation's years of work and sacrifices for
granted, and in this respect the Polish young people are like the
youth of any other country.

I closed my visit to Wroclaw with a stirring musical experience. Ignacy, now my friend as well as that of my brother, took me
to the State Opera to see a modern ballet based on an eastern
legend, entitled *The Song of Longing*. It was choreographed by
Adam Swierzynski, and its score and setting were by Lili Rot-
baum. The dancing was superb and kept us in a state of spiritual

tension which we later drowned in a restaurant with bison vodka, coffee, and a meal of *escalopes de veau a la Viennoise* and *mille feuilles Chantilly*.

Before I left the city, I received a special-delivery letter from my daughter, who had been accepted at a children's camp in Zakopane. She wrote:

> We have many activities such as sailing, canoeing, land sports, arts and crafts, folk singing, girls' and boys' dancing . . . a first aid class where I learned to treat injuries, as well as learning their scientific names. I also took my guitar to camp . . . practicing every free period and strumming very well. I hope to see you soon so I can play you some songs . . . am learning folk singing from my counselor.
>
> My cabin is very big. I room with seven girls and three counselors. We also have mice in our cabin because the girls carry a lot of food in their bags, even though it is not allowed in any cabin. The mice chewed up my pillowcase, a pair of shorts, and two other girls' sleeping bags. One mouse slept in one of the counselors' beds when she was asleep. One night the counselors put mice traps in the cabin. I didn't sleep all night. The two traps were put near my bed because the mice usually come to my corner. We caught two mice. I was so scared.
>
> The food here is very good. We have well-balanced meals and can have as much as we want. We cannot choose what we want to eat, but have to eat what is given. We don't have to eat everything on our plates though.
>
> Last Friday Mommy and Anthony came up to see me. After lunch, Anthony and I paddled in a canoe to the dam. Anthony managed to fall into the water and Mommy had to iron his clothes until they got dry. Afterwards, I took some little children in a rowboat.
>
> Yesterday we had Christmas in summer. Everyone had to give a present to someone else in the cabin. I gave a basket to one of the deaf girls in my cabin. There are two deaf girls in my cabin. They are wonderful. Very kind. They can speak, but their words are sometimes hard to understand. Both girls can hear very high and very low sounds. . . ."

Chapter 13

slow storks
*   fly low*
dragging frayed webs of wings
across the faded rainbow of the field

nor heart
nor meadow
can sustain this woe
unless hope yield
stout girdle banding them
with promised blossoming
for us
alack
there is no help save this
who hold today's forgetmenot
too close
for aught
but tragic song that lashes us
until repentance stings
*   o*
*   fellow men*
*   who have not even*
*   breathed*
*   of*
*   spring*

193

Despite the destruction of the Second World War, the past is everywhere in Poland: in her cities, towns, and villages; in Silesia, in the Lubusz territory, Szczecin Pomerania, Gdansk Pomerania; and in old Eastern Prussia (now known as Mazurian Pomerania). One of the most historical of these towns is Bolkow, which is located seventeen miles from Jelenia Gora. After making my way through winding streets and ancient buildings, I came upon a castle at the edge of town. It was built in the twelfth century by Prince Bolko, one of the descendants of King Boleslaw the Wrymouth, to house his lover, a beautiful girl whom he had kidnapped from Cracow under the very nose of another nobleman.

I could make out the defensive moats and deep trenches built to beat back the attacks of the Germans from the west. One of the German margraves had laid siege here in 1347 for eight months, but had to turn back after losing 1,500 men. Long, secret passageways set deeply underground led from this castle all the way across the town to another castle, the property of the Polish magnate Swinka. Around these two castles revolves the following romantic tale:

Prince Bolko had a son who fell in love with Swinka's daughter and wanted to marry her. The old man Swinka did not approve the match. When he learned that the pair was meeting in secret in defiance of his wishes, he ordered his servants to cast his daughter into a dungeon.

The maiden would have perished had it not been for young Bolko, who gave orders to have a passageway dug from his castle to Swinka's. Day and night his men dug. How long it took, legend does not say, but it was not too long, for when Bolko finally regained and embraced his sweetheart, she was still very much alive and as beautiful as ever.

The oldest part of the city is the marketplace. When I visited, it was summertime and the vine-covered porches of the old buildings provided us with an exquisite shade. A huge chestnut tree with its great spreading branches and mass of foliage stood in the very middle of the market, a living testimony to the days when these buildings were first erected.

A steep street leading out of the marketplace drops sharply into a ravine—the stony bed of a fast-moving, foaming river. It would be more proper to call it a stream, but in the springtime its waters once rose wildly and, imbued with terrible power, it destroyed everything around. That is how it earned its name—Wild Nisa. Today, confined within its strong manmade banks, it flows quietly along, keeping soberly within the space allotted it.

The marketplace of Bolkow has another point of interest: a small, thirteenth-century church, later named the Church of St. Jadwiga. At the rear wall of the church is an insignificant-looking cross. According to legend, when Bolkow was still heathen, a pagan god inhabited the town. He was the town patron and his worshippers came here to offer up sacrifices and prayers. When Christianity came to Bolkow and a church was built, a cross was placed on the same spot sacred to the pagan god. After their conversion, however, the natives yearned for their old religion and could not reconcile themselves to the new one. Many different times the cross was removed from the site of the ancient god, but it was always recovered. To this day, that small and solitary cross survives, a mute witness to the vicissitudes of the centuries.

At various periods in her history, Bolkow was known as Bolkoburg or Bolkenheim, reflecting its various foreign conquests. The twelfth-century name Bolkow was restored in 1945. It was always a Polish town, however, as evidenced by the fact that the objects exhibited in the museum of the castle date back to the tenth, eleventh, and twelfth centuries. The objects include wooden ploughs and armor from the old Slavic days; crests of the local Polish nobility; and battle standards and small stone figures of knights with the eagle of the Piasts carved on them.

As I stood in the church, staring at this small, stark cross, I thought of the last war, of how many people had fought and died—more than in any other war in all human history. Had the best perished?

Next on my agenda was Wolborz. Not far from this town is a palace where every year young people come from many parts of the world for their vacation. Besides being a place for dancing, singing, and all kinds of sports, its also gives them an opportunity to learn the language of their fathers, for all the languages of the world are spoken here. Everyone eventually dances well because dancing is the international language. A dance competition is held in the largest hall of the palace to which local officials and the general public are invited. After this competition, there is a feast and the rest of the night is spent talking and playing games. But this is an exceptional day—not all the days are spent dancing.

Living and learning in this eighteenth-century palace can be very pleasant, for it is surrounded by many trees and sports fields. Besides learning, the young people of this colony can go sightseeing and even visit distant places all over the country for historical, cultural, or artistic explorations. They are also visited by various Polish youth groups and workers' organizations. One of the most interesting experiences for them is a tour of coal mines or visits to Warsaw. The hosts show the foreign children every side of Polish live and have them participate in the same social and physical activities of Polish youth. There are approximately twenty such colonies for foreign children throughout Poland.

Lower Silesia is rich in a crystalline rock called magma, a molten rock material beneath the surface of the earth that is eventually transformed into igneous rock. Most precious is granite from which many Polish monuments are built, including the column of King Zygmunt standing on Castle Place in Warsaw. From the region of Szklarska Poreba, miners obtain a pink granite known all over Europe. In the region of Strzelin, the largest quarry in Europe is located, producing many varieties of commercial rock materials used in building roads.

Lower Silesia is the richest source of minerals in Poland. It produces beautiful sandstone as well as iron ore, copper, nickel, barite, kaolin, uranium, silver, and gold. Centuries ago, the largest gold mine in Europe was located here. From all over the world so many prospectors and adventurers came to get rich that the gold resources became exhausted by the fourteenth century. But even today in a place like Kaczow or Bobr, one can find the small pieces of gold that have become a great attraction for young people's summer excursions. The gold is usually mixed with ore of arsenopyrite which has no practical use. A huge quantity of this substance must be processed in order to extract a very small amount of the precious metal.

In recent years, Cepelia, the Polish trade association, has utilized the resources of Lower Silesia by organizing a small factory where nephrite and agate are polished. Nephrite rock has a long history. Even in ancient times, the possessor of this rock was thought to be lucky in love and in health. Amethyst is also found in Lower Silesia. According to an old superstition, if amethyst is held to the stomach, it will prevent drunkenness. Cepelia also processes opal and florite for sale to jewelers. The most expensive rock is beryl, which is occasionally found in granite rocks in Lower Silesia. Olivine, on the other hand, is found in abundance in basalt formations. Chrysolite, a rare rock variation found with olivine, is clear, bright, and green in color. From time to time, tourmaline is found in blue, red, green, brown, or black. Naturally, all these findings are sporadic and not systematized, so Cepelia is primarily dependent on private prospecting to supply it with such precious stones.

More precious than any metal are the hard-working people of this region. From the bus window on my way to the village of Niemaszchleba, in the region where the Oder and Nisa rivers meet, I saw well-tended orchards and farms. Next to me on the bus sat two women. I was momentarily distracted by their conversation.

"How many children do you have?" asked the first one.

"Six."

"And what are their ages?"

"Ten, nine, eight, seven, six, and five."

"And what's happened in the last four years?"

"Nothing. Four years ago we bought ourselves a television set."

When I reached this village with the long name whose literal meaning is "you have no bread," a very curious incident was taking place.

A week before, a pair of storks had tried to produce new

offspring in the barn in the middle of the village. The female was sitting on the eggs while the male flew to the meadow to catch some frogs for her. On his way back he hit a high-powered electrical line and died. The female sat for days without moving and without food. The village people decided to do something. It was at this moment that I appeared. They took a tall ladder from the village fire department, and a group of children were sent to the meadow to catch come frogs. Two teenage boys climbed up with the frogs and started feeding the mother stork. Thus began a ritual which became a daily affair for a large gathering. At the first session I met Czeslaw Brewerski, who was the owner of the local flour mill. I asked him how long he had lived in Niemaszchleba.

"I have been here since 1940," he responded. "Before then I was a prisoner of war in Stalag Three B on the other side of the Nisa River, but I was escorted here to work in the flour mill as a slave laborer. I had a difficult time getting used to twelve hours of steady work on only two poor meals a day, but I prayed that some day I would be able to stay in this village as a free man. When the German army started moving under the pressure of the approaching Soviet and Polish armies, the owner of the mill left for Germany. But I stayed. During the military action, the flour mill was almost completely destroyed, but with the help of the neighbors and the government I was able to rebuild it."

"How about this group of children around you—are they all yours?"

"Yes. I even got married here where my wife, as well as our children, were born. And when I am gone I hope they will take good care of the flour mill."

When, in February, 1945, the Soviet and Polish armies were still moving in the direction of Berlin, Polish slave laborers returned to their country. Two of the laborers were Stanislaw Kurzynski and his wife. On their way home they stopped in Niemaszchelba for a rest—and never left. Their house, which stands almost squarely in the village center, was freshly painted and had a new fence around it. When I walked inside, I found four bright, clean rooms. Mrs. Kurzynski told me, "You see, we are

still resting here, after so many years. Our children finished
school, our son got married and already has a young daughter, and
we are certainly not going to move from here.''
Mr. Kurzynski interrupted. ''No, we are not moving. I rebuilt
this badly damaged house. Look here through the window. I
planted the whole orchard garden. My original farm in the Poznan
district was completely destroyed and was taken by a landless
farmer's helper from eastern Poland. I was the first one here. Later
during the same year, twenty more farmers arrived from Germany
and we started working hard to rebuild the village.''
Gradually, Kurzynski became a village leader. Animal husbandry and fruit production were begun, and a school was built.
The first teacher was Captain Franek Biedrzynski, a former soldier
and inhabitant of a German concentration camp. The first students
to enroll were six-year-old Kasia Bielanska and Wojtek Bula. In
1973, Ms. Bielanska was a teacher in this same school and Mr.
Bula was the principal. The month following my visit they were
married.
The village grew to a hundred well-kept buildings, and on
half of the houses there were television antennas. The local general
store was full of domestic and foreign products, and in the fire-
house the villagers saw new films every week. When I visited the
local priest, he showed me a 200-year old record of christenings
and weddings; all the names were Polish. At the cemetery as well,
all the tombstones bore only Polish names. Some stones had been
partly damaged in the war, especially by the retreating Germans.
Two days later when I was leaving the village, the news
spread that a new male stork had appeared at the barn. This, of
course, created a great stir of excitement. Everyone rushe
there and found the stranger talking to the female, who was sti
sitting on her eggs. After their short conversation, the newcom
exchanged places with the female, and she flew to the mead
for a meal.
Storks are only one of the many kinds of birds in Pola
Twenty-two percent of the country is covered with forests
which are many different birds and animals. Hunters come

from all over the world, and Orbis, the Polish government travel bureau, organizes hunting expeditions. Hunting is one of the oldest sports in Poland. Kings, nobles, and even peasants have engaged in its pursuit for centuries.in the northern part of the country, superstiton still has it that a young boy cannot have his breakfast until he shoots a bird or a loaf of bread hanging from a tree.

In Western Europe only the rich can afford to have hunting territory, and often there isn't much game on these lands except rabbits. Every year thousands of European hares are sent to France from Poland. There they are released in hunting territories, and wardens bring the hunters to the appropriate areas in trucks to let them hunt. Most of the Bieszczady Region, and the Bialowieska, Borecka and Augustowska forests are still in their natural, virgin state, inhabited by stags, fallow deer, wild boars, roe deer, foxes, red deer, and lynx. According to facts collected by foresters, Poland has over 100,000 stags and about the same number of wild boars, 150,000 roe deers, and a million European hares. Orbis, recognizing that hunters are intérested in the atmosphere of the natural surroundings and in sportsmanship, books hunting expeditions well in advance. Although hunting takes place throughout the year for different animals, the most popular season is September, when the Polish wilderness echoes with the mating calls of the stags.

Another sport popular among both poles and foreign visitors in horseback riding. Horse training is 400 years old in Poland, and in the state horse stables can be found some of the best stallions in the world. Every year Polish horses are sold to Great Britain, Holland, Sweden, Italy, Switzerland, and even to Egypt, Canada, and the United States. Not surprisingly, Polish horses under Canadian colors won at the International Competition in 1963, and five years later, the Polish breed Aron won the competition as Holland's best horse.

Poland has ten centers of horse husbandry which are open to foreign visitors during the summer. Here they have the privilege of selecting horses and instructors. Beginners are exposed to inte

sive training in the nearby fields and parks, and the advanced riders take long excursions and may even stay overnight in distant inns and motels.

In my travels around the country, I reached Koszalin, a city situated not far from the Baltic Sea. Koszalin originated in the twelfth century as a fishing village and in the following century came under burgher law. During the Second World War, it was completely destroyed. It took many years to rebuild it to the standards of historical perfection set in Poland's other reconstructed cities. Not far from Koszalin is a little town called Bialy Bor, which is located in the forest among hills that look out over a picturesque lake—ideal terrain for horse riding. A complex of buildings here house over 100 stallions, attendants, and guests. There is also a special trotting arena protected by a roof, as well as an open field for horse training. Jodphur breeches and high boots are familiar dress in this part of the country, as French, English, and Polish are exchanged among the guests. Early in the morning, horses can be seen galloping, jumping, and trotting, and they seem to be as happy as the riders because they are well fed and cared for. The afternoon starts with riding in all kinds of carriages— American, Hungarian, and Polish—that travel along the field roads. The morning is for the young riders, the afternoon for the middle-aged and old people.

In my visit there I met a very pleased New York City travel-agency owner who told me that from now on he would be organizing horse tours in Poland.

"I think you will make lots of money," I commented optimistically.

"I think I will too. Everybody is so helpful, and they offered me a substantial bonus for setting up tours."

"There are more good people than smart ones."

"What do you mean by that?" he asked.

"It is easier to imitate a good man than a smart one."

Not far from the town of Ustka, which is northeast of Koszalin almost on the Baltic Sea, I witnessed a Polish meteorological rocket launching. The preparation took three years. The rocket named ''Meteor'' was over eight feet long and reached an altitude of twenty-two miles. As I learned from my conversation with an engineer from the Institute of Aviation, the Poles were working on several more high flights. One of the engineers told me with a smile, ''I am sure that some day we will reach the heavens and the Assumption.''

Chapter 14

With slow and gilded motion
Across the blue of space
Go clouds in velvet glory
In snow-radiant, golden chase.

Drawn from the earthen quiver
The swallow, sharp and slender,
Slips like a silvered arrow
Against the sunmail splendor.

A rainbow frame encircles
The calm and shining meadow;
Within the darkeyed brooks
Float flakes of golden shadow.

And down through the dim, green forest
Like grass tongues, pours its lustre,
Or flutters in the branches
Its winging, burning clusters.

On skies, on fields, on forests,
Evading all pursuit,
The great sun, high over the blue path,
Hangs like a ripening fruit.

—Kazimierz Przerwa-Tetmajer

Probably the most picturesque region in all of Poland is the two northeastern provinces, Warmia and Mazury, an area of 2,700 lakes and many forests. Many years ago, the Suchodolski brothers laid plans to connect the lakes by means of canals to allow for the transportation of agricultural goods and other products as well as to facilitate communications. Today, it is the ideal place for tourists. On the small islands and on the edges of the lakes nest wild ducks, cormorants, wild geese, swans, and other birds. In the lakes there are fish, and in the forests I saw bison, elk, and an animal similar to the musk ox called *tarpan* in Polish.

One of the most delightful aspects of life in Poland is that all this beauty can be had without the harassment of "No Trespassing" signs and license fees. Nor is the tourist ever disturbed by the sight of refuse strewn about. I marveled at the extent to which people went camping and at the lushness of the camp sites. Holiday boarding houses dot the country and accommodations have increased sixfold since 1960 to well over 400,000 vacancies. The government provides reduced railway fares for workers on holiday and has increased its expenditures on worker vacations by 30 percent.

Before the Second World War, blue collar workers' holidays could not by law exceed fifteen calendar days a year. Today, a worker receives that amount of paid vacation time after his first year of work and twenty-six of these days after ten years of labor. This is in addition to the usual holidays and paid time off for education.

In addition to the workers who frequent Warmia and Mazury, every year thousands of foreign tourists come. The government, seizing the potential for profit, has built motels in these provinces. Although they are on main roads, they still afford access to the wildlife in this part of the country. The most popular tourist sights are the lakes, especially Sniardwy, Mazury, Kisajny, and Niegocinskie. These lakes form a long line of exquisite sights, providing enjoyment for tourists and local citizens alike.

One group of Mazurian towns, among them Elk, Ketrzyn, Gizycko, Wegorzewo, and Mikolajki, has many historical monuments. The Ketrzyn Museum, for example, contains rare books printed in the Gothic alphabet as well as old paintings. Also found there is the work of Wojciech Ketrzynski, who, according to the plaque in the museum, was born in 1838 in Gizycko as Adalbert von Winkler. During his school years, he discovered that he was Polish and that his father had changed his name from the Polish to insure a career and to protect him from the Germans. As a result, young Wojciech embarked on a lifetime of research, study, travel, and writing on Polish enthnography and history. He also kept in contact with other Polish writers such as the novelist I. J. Kraszewski and the Nobel-Prize-winning novelist Henryk Sienkiewicz. In 1945, the town where he lived and worked was named after him.

Not far from Ketrzyn, Hitler's underground forts can still be seen, together with well-fortified houses and hotels for the S. S. men. In the neighboring town of Karolewo are buildings that served as concentration camps in which the S.S. men tortured Russian and Polish prisoners of war. Today, in the buildings which were not destroyed, there is an agricultural school. The ruins have been preserved to remind the young students of the tragedy which this territory experienced during the Second World War.

In another town, Swieta Lipka, or "The Sacred Linden Tree," there is a beautiful monastery with a baroque church. The history of this church is connected with the legend of a linden tree and the Holy Mother who rested beneath it and afterwards asked some Polish noblemen to build a church there. To commemorate this event, a golden chalice was fashioned in the exquisitely crafted shape of a linden tree. It is still highly revered by the people.

The main gates to the church were made of iron in the seventeenth century. They are so delicately designed that one would guess they were made by a special artist rather than by local blacksmiths who made the pattern out of a design of trees and flowers. Inside the church are many beautiful old paintings and frescoes.

Another town with historical landmarks is Malbork, which has a huge castle and fortifications that date back to the thirteenth century when the Teutonic Knights were headquartered there. During the fourteenth and fifteenth centuries, this town and its neighboring territories witnessed many bloody combats between the local Polish people and the German invaders. From the middle of the fifteenth century, this part of the country was restored to Poland, and the castle hosted Polish kings. The castle has been meticulously restored and is one of many fine tourist attractions.

Northeast of Malbork, not far from the Baltic's dark waters, is a fishing town named Frombork which has a fifteenth-century Gothic cathedral. In the church adjacent to this cathedral, Mikolaj Kopernik (Nickolas Copernicus) established his famous astronomical observatory in 1497. Here, too, he died on May 24, 1543, and was buried beneath the cathedral's floor. Frombork has the world's only Copernican Museum.

The capital of the provinces of Warmia and Mazury is the city of Olsztyn. Here there is an agricultural school which is perhaps the only one in Europe that provides an engineering degree in dairy science. A Gothic cathedral, the city hall, and the high gates are witnesses to this city's past glory. From these gates Copernicus directed the defense of Olsztyn in 1521 against the attacking German crusaders. As you walk through the city's spacious, lush parks and gardens, you can experience the harmony between the old architecture and the new. The people of these provinces derive their income from agriculture, tobacco, and fishing. The houses of the farmers are small but neat and whitewashed; most of them are located on the edge of a lake. Everywhere there are birds, trees, and flowers. On my last visit in 1975, I entered one of the houses, scaring chickens and geese with my brisk walk. I explained to the woman who owned the farm that I was born on a farm and had come to refresh my memory and renew my acquaintance.

She smiled and said, "Please, sit down."

Before I had a chance to say more, she disappeared. In a few minutes she returned telling me that she had gone to the cellar to get something. She then placed a jar of fresh buttermilk, black bread, butter, and cheese on the white cloth-covered table. "You have probably come quite a distance. Please have something to eat."

I thanked her for her kindness and asked her about her family.

"My husband, together with our two sons, is in the field.

They will be back shortly. Our sons are studying agriculture in college. Right now they are on vacation and are helping their father. We also have a daughter. She is married to a policeman and lives in Olsztyn.''

"Only three children?'' I said with mock disappointment in my voice.

She smiled, displaying a gold tooth, "Do you want to know everything right away?''

Before I could reply, she added, "Two other younger boys are twins and work in a different part of the field. One watches the cows and the other geese. And I have one more, but I sent him to the store to buy a kilogram of sugar and some other things I need. Tomorrow my daughter is coming with her husband and I would like to bake a cake and surprise them.''

"So you have six children.''

"Yes, and all of them were born here,'' she said, getting up to open the door since she saw her boy through the window, returning with an armload of groceries from the store.

At his side was a small boy.

"But you said you only have six children?''

"This one is my grandson.'' The woman was obviously pleased that I had thought the child was also hers.

She then presented me to this tiny fellow with light hair and black eyes. "He is named Edward Gierek Jankowski, after our First Secretary. He is so smart that someday he too will be a leader of our country.''

"That's very nice.'' I stretched my hand out to the boy.

"That is not true; and I am not so smart.'' he replied, squeezing my hand. "I don't know why you keep saying I'll be the leader.''

Here the woman added: "He was given this name because we owe everything to Mr. Gierek and his leadership.''

"You cannot be grateful to just one person,'' interjected her son. "Lots of other people are responsible for creating a better life for our country, including we ourselves.''

"I don't know too much about politics,'' said the woman. "My husband and I were slave laborers in Bavaria, and when we returned here the Polish government told us, 'Here is the farm and let's see what you can do.' And sir, you can see for yourself what we did with only our hands—we rebuilt everything.''

"It's not true," said the boy. "The government gave you the seeds to plant and a loan to build the house, and the neighbors helped you during the first harvest as well as helping to build the barn when you were expecting a baby and when father had a broken leg——''

"That's true," agreed the woman with irritation in her voice. "The neighbors and government helped us and for that reason I pray for them every day.''

"Mother, are your shoes hurting you?''

"Why?'' asked the woman, looking rather bewildered.

"Oh, nothing, because Grandfather said many times that when you put on tight shoes you forget everything.''

After I left the farm, I came upon another village where the houses were covered with red shingles and were hidden among gardens.

"Where is Sobolewski's house?'' I asked a farmer who was passing by.

"Franciszek or Boleslaw?''

"I really don't know; but who is the better farmer?''

"Both of them are good, but I think you want Franciszek. His home is behind the school.''

It took me five minutes to reach the house. My first sight was of a clean triangular courtyard with barking dogs and strutting chickens, turkeys, and geese all around. I was immediately confronted by a gray-haired lady in her late sixties, who after greeting me announced that her son was in Olsztyn and would be back shortly.

"Yes, of course, I came to see your son, but I would also like to see your farm, which is known in the neighborhood for its productivity.''

The old lady had strong working hands. She smiled and asked me to follow her. As soon as I entered her home, I smelled freshly baked bread and pastry.

"This is my daughter-in-law," she said as she introduced a tall, young woman in her thirties. "She's the expert baker in the family."

The young woman smiled calmly and said, "You should have a mother-in-law like mine."

The five-room house was plain, but the tables, beds, and chest of drawers were hand-carved and well-polished. The kitchen and bath towels were hand-sewn, and the flowers on the living room table were freshly cut from the garden. The pots and pans were so bright that the copper shone like a mirror. The Muzurian people are lovers of order and harmony, a sentiment which is especially reflected in their beautiful handicrafts. When I went outside, I observed that the agricultural machinery was as clean and as polished as the kitchen pots. I also noticed the same polish on the ten black-and-white cows which were grazing near the fence bordering the meadow. Most private farmers in other parts of Poland don't bother brushing their cows. Sometimes they brush the horses out of a sense of pride rather than for the comfort of the horse. Indeed, many a Polish farmer is accused of loving his horse more than his wife.

Suddenly, a spry man in his seventies appeared and, with a smile revealing worn-down teeth, said, "I am Franciszek. My son will be home very soon."

"You have a very well-kept farm," I said.

"Yes, I do," he replied. "We work very hard here." Turning around he continued, "I would like to introduce you to my guest. His name is Wilhelm."

"A German?" I asked.

"Yes," he replied, "a German who speaks only a few words of Polish, but who knows English very well, as you shall see."

"How did he learn English?"

"We met during the First World War," said Wilhelm changing the subject in broken Polish. He was the same size as Franciszek, though a little heavier with a mustache. He could have been Franciszek's younger brother.

"Yes, we met on the front during the First World War,"

confirmed Franciszek. "I was ready to bayonet him and he was ready to fire on me with his gun. Instead, we both smiled, I dropped my empty gun, and he dropped his loaded one."

"And now," said Wilhelm, "we visit each other every year."

"You know, Wilhelm's only son was killed on the eastern front during the last war."

Here the German farmer shook his hand and said, "I enjoy spending six weeks on his farm, and I hope he enjoys staying on mine, although he doesn't like my daughter-in-law."

Our conversation was interrupted when Franciszek's son drove his old automobile into the courtyard. Wilhelm observed, "You see, if you have money, you can buy yourself a car, but if you have no money, you die normally." We all started laughing.

His host commented playfully, "You are jealous, Wilhelm. Although you haven't got a car, you know well enough how to drive."

"It's true that I don't have a car, and I don't have a wife, yet I know how to take care of a woman."

At this moment, young Sobolewski joined us, and the four of us went into the house to eat.

After the first toast and while we were eating pickled herring with onion, old Sobolewski resumed talking, asking me about the United States. His interest was personal because, although he himself had never been there, his older brother had spent a few years in New York working for the pianist Paderewski. Among other questions, Franciszek asked me, "Is Mr. Harriman still alive?"

"There are many Harrimans in the United States. Do you mean W. Averell Harriman, the millionaire, ex-playboy, and diplomat?"

"I don't know, but does this man play polo and the piano?"

"When he was a young man he did many things," I said, reaching for a third piece of herring with onion and putting it on a chunk of black bread. I then began to tell him my less than polite story about Harriman, which I had heard secondhand from the industrialist John D. Biggers.

"During the Second World War, when Harriman was appointed to the War Production Board, his superior, the powerful William S. Knudsen, didn't approve the appointment because he didn't believe playboys made good workers. On one of Harriman's first days on the job, Knudsen called him into his office and warned him. 'I don't believe that you will ever quit "butterflying" or being a "playboy," but I am under pressure to accept you. Now you're in a position to disprove my point.' "

"This must be the same Harriman," the old Sobolewski said. "My brother said that at one reception for Paderewski, Harriman decided to play Chopin, to which the great musician was forced to listen. My brother said that after the reception the illustrious host asked Paderewski what he thought about Harriman's playing, and he replied, 'Averell is a dear soul who plays polo, and I am a mere Pole who plays solo.' "

"It's true," said Wilhelm, slowly sipping his vodka. "The Americans think they are entitled to do everything because they are rich, and look at the mess they have brought to the world."

The elder Sobolewski leaned toward me and said, "Wilhelm comes from West Germany, and he believes that American big business is preparing the Germans and the Japanese for a third world war. And who knows, maybe some of Harriman's interests are there too."

"It will be very difficult," said his son. "Today Poland is different from the Poland before the Second World War. Not only are there popular will and arms to defend Polish soil, but we also have powerful allies."

"It will be good," said the father, "if we can put the warmongers in the crazy house." Then he paused to scratch his bald head, "But I don't think we can. If we could put them there, though, I'm sure no sensible doctor would let them out."

Chapter 15

even the stolid hills
                    stretch out their arms
to take
        the stammering stream
        as i would you
now when as the pines' green needles run the sunset through
                            and
                            pierce
                    bright silence
                        with

            an
        emerald
            cry
    a heart ungiven
    seeks you
    in breathless depths
    stifles in loves
    first longing

                            what whim
                            of god
                            decreed your name
                            made you a woman
                            not windlifted flame

The simplicity and charm of the ordinary people and the countryside renewed my love for my native land. My longing for my children and wife, whom I had left in Zakopane, intensified this love.

I returned to Warsaw with a rather comprehensive collection of photographs from my trip around the country. My family was also there, having ended their pleasant stay in Zakopane. At our first supper together, they presented me with their own collection of photographs. My mother, now greatly improved in health, had also come, along with my three brothers and their families. Mother had prepared a fine meal consisting of strawberry soup, mushrooms with cream, chicken, potatoes, and a cucumber salad. We topped off the meal with the famous Warsaw pastries and Chinese tea. My older brother presented me with a box of Polish cigars called *Pro Patria* which were manufactured at the Koscianska Tobacco Factory; they tasted like good Cuban cigars. A package of five cigars cost only twenty *zlotys* and fifty *grosze*, which is less than a dollar.

Even with the windows and the door to the balcony open, the house was filled with smoke and the sounds of laughter. We were trying to solve some minor problems, such as whether we should have four children each or be satisfied with the ones we already had. We also ventured into national and international politics, which, with the help of a good meal and a good cigar, always seems to be soluble in good conversation. We discussed the United States and the possibility of a third world war. This was the saddest part of our last evening together. We felt helpless. Our final conclusion was that life, as one Polish writer has written, is like a child's undershirt—short and full of shit.

Our pessimistic dialogue was interrupted by my sixteen-year-old nephew Rysiek, who expressed optimism for the future of his country and the world. He berated us harshly. "You old people, if you cannot be more encouraging about the future, you might as well shut up."

He continued. "Don't you see around you that every day there is more food in stores, new houses are being built, new roads

paved. There is new hope. The youth of Poland do not want to hate
anyone anymore, not even the Germans. If you don't believe your
eyes, you might at least believe in statistics. Can't you understand
all this?'' Then he began citing the statistics, but numbers have
always wearied me. So I excused myself politely and went to bed.

The next morning I was awakened by the light streaming
through the window. I lay there thinking how

> the sun lavishes all
> the heart with light
>   that falls
> in multiple hues
>   unstinted
love in the breast
shall top our
highflung walls
>   crimeladen
>   let us
>   rest
>   in infinite fields of earth
>   with flowering worlds imprinted
>   let eyes
>   in eyes
>   once look
>   with different gaze
>   look full
love in the breast
must top our
highflung walls

We heard a voice melodiously calling out: "Strawberries,
blueberries! Strawberries! Blueberries!" I peered through the
window and saw a tall woman with a brightly colored kerchief on
her head and a matching skirt covering her big behind. She was
also wearing a white blouse with red embroidered flowers on her

sleeves. On both arms she carried baskets full of strawberries and blueberries. Children were coming towards her to buy berries. Near the building two men in white uniforms pushed a green cart full of milk bottles which they were distributing to the various apartments. On all four sides of the courtyard were four huge sandboxes; because of the early hour, instead of children, pigeons were playing. The early morning sun shone over clusters of flowers in the center of the courtyard, which a blue-suited janitor was watering with a long hose.

Our stay in Poland was coming to an end. Rather than idle in bed, I went directly to the phone and called Orbis to reserve four seats on the Moscow-Rome train which passed through Warsaw every evening. Unhappily, I was informed that only two seats were available. But the pleasant woman at Orbis told me that we could have four seats on a Lot jet and that tickets for the three-hour trip from Warsaw to Rome would cost $104 per person.

After I made the reservations, I had breakfast with my family, and then we took my mother outside to the monument dedicated to the heroes of the Warsaw Jewish ghetto, before which we took some snapshots. We took a last walk around the capital. As the workday was beginning, the streets were crowded. In the morning sun everything looked new and fresh. Suddenly, despite the morning's splendor, I had a poignant vision of how Warsaw must have looked after the war with stumps of buildings and ruined, ashen heaps of destroyed churches and houses. I turned to my mother who seemed to be sharing my vision. To prevent unnecessary unhappiness, I asked Anthony and Gloria to take their grandmother to the Europejski Hotel where we were later to have lunch with the rest of the family and some close friends. We continued walking until we reached Constitution Square. I noticed that Sophia too looked sad, and I asked her what was troubling her.

"It's difficult to define. I'm not thinking about anything," she said, hoping I'd drop the subject.

"How can you think about nothing when you have seen so many new things and a country of such hard-working people?"

"I'm overwhelmed," she began again, but said no more.

At this moment we were in front of a huge window of the Cepelia store, where folk arts and crafts were displayed. Here tourists were buying handsome carpets and tapestries, amber and silver broaches, beads and rings, wooden sculptures, glossy ceramic vases, and regional peasant garments from the Carpathian mountains and the Cracow and Lowicz districts. These garments are hand-woven and hand-embroidered. Although these costumes are basically similar in concept, they differ with respect to the individual craftsmanship that goes into each work. Short or three-quarter-length fur coats and jackets with embroidered collars are popular among young Europeans. The older people favor hand-made silver jewelry, icons, and old paintings. Government experts are present in the store and willingly give advice on the art objects.

After browsing around the store, I bought an amber necklace for Sophia, the latest Polish recording of Chopin for Gloria, and, for Anthony, a recording of the two famous song-and-dance groups Slask and Mazowsze, both of whom we had seen in New York.

The next day was again sunny. Warsaw was in a holiday spirit. Displayed on her streets were red-and-white flags (the national colors of Poland) and flowers wherever you looked. It was July 22, the day of liberation and the most important national holiday of the year. Driving in a taxi through the city for the last time, we saw thousands of people in their best clothes, some of them scurrying to take part in the parade, others just watching. Music was all around us. Against the backdrop of a perfectly blue sky, flocks of pigeons moved in all directions, chaotically yet seemingly keeping time to the music. It was our last look at Warsaw.

At ten o'clock we arrived at Okecie Airport, which also sparkled with red-and-white flags and flowers. We were leaving with four valises filled with gifts. The other twelve we had left with my relatives. When the customs officials asked us what we had in our luggage, I simply said, "Personal." As on the day we entered Poland, their response was simply, "Thank you and have a pleasant trip."

A young girl in the bluish-gray uniform of LOT Airlines ran over to Gloria, who was already by the ramp of the plane, and pinned a red carnation on her dress. Gloria started crying, and the girl began talking to her and hugging her at the same time. The loud, numbing sound of the engines drowned out their farewell, and all I could see was their moving lips.

As soon as we were settled in our seats, Gloria unpinned the carnation and placed it in the center of an English book of poems about Poland and her thousandth year of existence as a state. Her uncle Marion had given her the book as a parting gift.

From time to time, I still see Gloria looking through this book; the flower has lost none of its shape nor its color.

Epilogue

MOREK

now
when moths fly
their
soundless nightly round
over
my rest in
a nocturnal spell
i
make my vow

never
will i deny
this
luminous hope
this
deep revolt
make
black hypocrisy
my
cause

i know too well
not all this blood
will drench one pocket
with gold
these billion mothers cries
are not the last
to smell the criminal
air

my raveled heart goes
streaming to the mold
and some october in
the autumn cold
when nature grieving in
her purple robes
with wiry thorn probes
the marrowless bone
picks
at
the shriveled heart
                ill
                shout
                aloud
                its
                i

i yield no shred of my revolt to be plucked out
still unforgiving
and remembering
the ultimate deceit
of gun and
              knout
beauty inflamed
beyond their power to dim
morning remains
                    i
                    will be born
                    again
                    for all their
                    pains
                    through love will
                    rise
                    to lash with
                    living
                    faith
                    words the voiceless
                    of stricken men
                    possess
                    them drive them
                    on
                    that by this
                    ache
                    of mine
          this longing forged in
          every battle crash
          their hearts shall be
          made whole
          to
                    free forever mans partitioned soul